Company and Business Records for Family Historians

by

Eric D. Probert

FEDERATION OF FAMILY HISTORY SOCIETIES

Published by
The Federation of Family History Societies
The Benson Room, Birmingham and Midland Institute
Margaret Street, Birmingham B3 3BS

Copyright © Eric D. Probert

First published 1994

ISBN 0-872094-92-9

Printed by and bound by Oxuniprint, Walton Street, Oxford OX2 2DP

£3.95

Contents

Acknowledgements

My thanks are due to the staff in the many record repositories that have been contacted and visited for their valuable assistance in providing information for the preparation of this booklet. To Derek Palgrave for his encouragement and to Cliff and Jean Debney for reading the draft and providing helpful comments.

This booklet is deicated to my Mother, the late Winifred Probert, whose own thirst for knowledge inspired me to write it.

I am also grateful to a number of Record Repositories for permission to publish extracts from documents in their collections as examples of the wide range of source material available to family historians.

In particular, I wish to acknowledge the following organisations for giving permission to reproduce the figures:

Society of Genealogists, figure 1.
Essex Record Office, figures 2, 3, 5, 6, 8 and 11-14.
National Register of Archives, figure 4.
Gloucestershire County Record Office, figure 7.
Herefordshire and Worcester County Record Office, figure 9.
Birmingham Central Library: Archives Division, figure 10.
National Westminster Bank: Group Archives, figures 15 and 16.
Public Record Office, figures 17-21.
Companies House, figures 22-24.
Post Office Archives and Record Centre, figure 25.
Controller of Her Majesty's Stationary Office, figure 26.
Cadbury Ltd: Library and Archives. figure 27.

List of Figures

14. Samuel Courtauld and Company, Essex, Register of Employment of Young Persons (1912).
15. London & County Banking Co., Register of Officers at Head Office and Branches (1868 to 1908), Chelmsford 1868-9
16. London & County Banking Co., Signature Book of the Chelmsford, Essex, Branch of the 1880's.
17. Chelmsford Corn Exchange Company, Essex, Memorandum of Association, 1857, giving details of Initial Subscribers.
18. Chelmsford Corn Exchange Company, Essex, List of Shareholders from the 1858 Annual Return.
19. Women's Aerial League of the British Empire, Memorundum of Association, 1909. List of original Subscribers.
20. General drapery business, 'Annette' of Shenfield, Essex, Form of Registration, 1931.
21. Thomas Tapling & Co. Limited, Yiewsley, Middlesex, Petition to the Chancery Division of the High Court of Justice, 1943.
22. Humphries & Taplings Ltd, Yiewsley, Middlesex, Packet in which microfiched records are presented from Companies House.
23. Humphries & Taplings Ltd, Yiewsley, Middlesex. List of Creditors, 1986.
24. Yiewsley Carpet Company, Middlesex. Share Allotment, 1950.
25. Post Office Establishment Book, 1891, reference to I. Probert.
26. Patent Application No. 18,935 (1895-6).
27. Cadbury Brothers Ltd, Extract from Girl's Register No. 4.
28. The Gas Light and Coke Company, House Journal, 'Co-partners' Magazine', 1944.

1. *Introduction*

This booklet explores the potential information on our ancestors that may exist in the surviving records of companies and similar organisations. The contents are relevant whether or not you already know that a person whose life you are researching was connected with a business.

The booklet examines ways of finding out about the existence of companies and businesses from the 19th Century onwards, looks at the means of locating where surviving records have been deposited, identifies the major repositories, provides a number of examples of the records that may be found and concludes with a reference section with useful addresses and further reading.

Occupations of persons from entries in the Census Returns and birth marriage and death certificates can give clues to a possible connection with a business. However, even if you have no evidence linking an ancestor or the subject of your research to a business it can be worthwhile examining the locality in which they lived during the period of their adult life to see what shops, banks, building societies, trading companies and other businesses were in existence, you can then go on to discover whether records have survived and if so search them.

The survival of business records is not very high since before the 1930's there was little preservation as such archives were generally not recognised as the valuable historical documents that they are today. As an example, of the 245 pages of the Guide to Gloucestershire Archives, only 17 are devoted to records of businesses which have been deposited. This figure is somewhat misleading, however, since deposits by solicitors, which include records of businesses such as trusts and insurance companies, account for a further 55 pages. There is a reasonable chance that you may find the subject of your research in business records as the person may have fulfilled any one or more of the roles of owner, director, investor, shareholder, manager, employee, customer or client, borrower, creditor and supplier of goods and services. With luck, you may find detailed information on the employment, character, personality, lifestyle and even health of your subject which may not have been gained in any other way.

Bear in mind that many companies will either have ceased trading, and been dissolved if they were registered, or have changed their name because they had been taken over or merged with other companies. It is therefore important to use the indexes to companies that have dissolved or changed name which are described in Chapter 3.

The author's own knowledge and experience is limited to companies in England and Wales but similar strategies may be employed for Scotland and Ireland using the relevant offices and sources for these countries.

2. *Finding out about Companies that existed*

Directories

The 'Trade' and 'Commercial' Sections of Post Office, Kellys and other County and City Directories are an excellant source for information on the existence of businesses from the 18th Century onwards and even earlier for large towns and cities. As an example, Lionel Frank PROBERT was described as a 'Raquet Maker' on his marriage Certificate of 1908 living in Stoke Newington and reference to the P.O. London Directory of 1908, page 2468, lists 11 possible employers under the heading of 'Raquet Makers'. Those nearest to where he lived, and therefore the most likely, being Mrs Wm Horton, T.H. Prosser & Sons and J. & S. Sheffield. Illustrated is an extract from Kelly's Directory of Gloucestershire for the town of Newnham-on-Severn, showing the large number of people in business listed in the 'Commercial' Section (*see figure 1*).

A 'Directory of Directors', a listing of the Directors of Joint Stock Companies of the United Kingdom, has been published annually since 1880 by Thomas Skinner and Company of London. The alphabetical listing normally includes the name, address and name(s) of the companies of which the person was a Director. It is interesting to note that the 1881 edition included 7,500 persons but that just 50 years later in 1931 the number of persons who were Directors had grown rapidly to 31,000.

Telephone Directories

Telephone directories were produced for London from 1881 and the provinces from 1900. These give alphabetical listings of private subscribers and all businesses by area. Back issues of these telephone directories will be found in some libraries and British Telecom Archives has an almost complete set of back issues in it's London search room which is open to the public by appointment (*see chapter 6*).

PRIVATE RESIDENTS.
Barnard Miss, Hope villa
Baillie Rev. William Gordon M.A. (vicar), The Vicarage
Balfour Henry T
Barling William
Barling William Cleophas
Boisier Edwd. Sandford, Highfield vils
Carleton John Shaw, Manor house
Carter Maurice Frederic, Banksian ho
Crawshay William J.P. Hyde
Dewey Rev. Herbert (Congregational)
Dredge Richard William
Fox Thomas Barker, Wistaria house
Gold Alfred Ernest
Guise John Wright, Highfield villas
Hadingham Stephen Wallace, Red ho
Hardeman John
Harrison H. M. Staunton, Highfield villas
Hinton William Henry, The Bank
Hunt Mrs
Jones Mrs. Highfield villas
Jones Mrs. William, Highfield villas
Kerr Russell James J.P. The Haie
Kerr Russell James, jun. J.P. Culver house
Langdon Mrs
Lloyd Francis Montagu, Duncombe
Lucas Frederick Lewis
Montefiore Mrs. Thomas Law, The Old Vicarage house
Parker Andrew, The Cliff
Probert Joseph
Roberts William George
Shiles John, Underhill
Thomas Arnold J.P. Severn Bank Lo
Wintle Douglas Jas. The Old house
Woods Saml. Wilkinson, The Beeches

COMMERCIAL.
Akerman Thomas Spring, butcher

Arnold George, gardener to Russell J. Kerr esq J.P
Baghurst George, farmer, Mutlows fm
Bailey Eliza (Mrs.), shopkeeper
Bailey John, coal merchant & goods agent to Gt. Western Railway Co
Barling William, farmer
Barling William Cleophas M.R.C.V.S. vet. surgeon
Barnard John, farm bailiff to Russell J. Kerr. J.P. Arams farm
Barnes Albert, hair dresser
Bevan Jane (Miss), apartments
Biggs James Boulton, inspector of weights & measures to the Gloucestershire County Council, Forest of Dean & Stroud divisions
Birks Emma (Mrs.), Railway inn & blacksmith, Bullo
Blanton Albert, plumber, painter & shopkeeper
Blanton Mary (Mrs.), earthenware dlr
Bluett Edmund, beer retailer, New Zealand inn
Brown Sydney Oscar, Prudential Insurance agent
Button Frederick, gamekeeper to Jas. Russell Kerr esq J.P
Cadle Thomas, auctioneer & estate agent & yeoman, Court farm, Westbury-on-Severn. See advert
Capital & Counties Bank Limited (branch) (William H. Hinton, manager); draw on head office, 39 Threadneedle street, London E C
Carefield John George, commission agent & assistant overseer & surveyor to local board
Carefield John James, deputy registrar of births & deaths, Newnham district & clerk to Churcham & Bulley school boards

Carleton John Shaw L.R.C.P.I. & L.R.C.S.I. medical officer & public vaccinator for No. 2 district, Westbury-on-Severn union, certifying factory surgeon & deputy sub-registrar Westbury-on-Severn district, medical officer to fever hospital, Soudley & surgeon captain to No. 7 Battery Gloucestershire Artillery Volunteers, Manor house
Carter Maurice Frederic, solicitor, clerk to magistrates, to the urban sanitary authorities of Awre, Newnham & Westbury-on-Severn, & to the guardians & rural sanitary authorities, & assessment committee of the Westbury-on-Severn union, to the commissioners of taxes for Newnham & Coleford division & vestry clerk to Westbury-on-Severn, coroner for the Forest division & superintendent registrar of Westbury-on-Severn district
Cemetery (Maurice Frederic Carter, clerk to the burial board)
Clarke Thomas, town crier
Clifford Elizabeth (Miss), rope maker
Cook George Chester, fishmonger
County Court (His Honor Arthur Beecher Ellicott, judge; John Wright Guise, registrar & acting high bailiff), Town hall
Cummings, Son & Co. saddlers & harness makers (branch)
Elton George, boot & shoe maker
Evans William, coal agent
Ferris Jas. harbour master, Bullo Pill
Fire Brigade (Volunteer) (Tom Simmons, captain)
Fluck Benjamin, farmer, Ruddle
Fox John August Adam William, watch maker

Figure 1. Kelly's Directory, extract for Newnham-on Severn, Gloucestershire, 1894.

Local Newspapers

Newspapers carried advertisements and County Record Offices and Libraries have holdings as well as the National Newspaper Library at Colindale, London. An extract from the front page of the 3rd January 1873 issue of the Chelmsford Chronicle is shown (*see figure 2*). Although with the reduction in size required for this publication it is difficult to read it is still possible to read the names of a variety of businesses both local and further afield.

Almanacs and Handbooks

Many trade, professional and commercial Institutions and Associations produced annual directories or handbooks listing the names and addresses of members. For instance, a publication listing all the banks in towns and cities and their senior officials and managers, the *Banking Almanac and Directory* has been published since 1845 and is a useful source for determining what banks were operating in a locality.

Parish Magazines

Introduced in the mid-19th Century a number have survived, and been deposited in local record offices, and often carry advertisements for businesses in the locality. Illustrated is an example from a Brightlingsea, Essex Parish Magazine of 1894 (*see figure 3*).

History Societies and their Publications

The Members of these Societies often have a detailed knowledge of the businesses that existed in a locality and sometimes the history of a business will feature in their publications. For example, The Birmingham & District Association of Local History Societies produces a Journal entitled *The Birmingham Historian* and Issue number 5 included an article *Women in Birmingham Factories*, which includes references to personal names.

Your local library, the British Association for Local History or the *Directory of British Associations* should be able to provide you with a contact in the Society for the area which interests you.

There are also specialist societies such as the Brewery History Society and the Railway & Canal Historical Society, which is dedicated to the

IRON WORKS, BROOMFIELD - ROAD, CHELMSFORD.

FELL CHRISTY,

GENERAL ENGINEER, MILLWRIGHT, IRON AND BRASS FOUNDER,

DESIRES to return Thanks to his numerous Customers for their patronage, and begs to state that, having made EXTENSIVE ADDITIONS to his Premises and Machinery, and Employing the Largest Staff of Millwrights in the county, is prepared to Supply all kinds of

CORN MILL MACHINERY

On Reasonable Terms, and with Despatch.

F. C. having been practically engaged in the Trade nearly 30 years, is prepared to Guarantee the Efficiency of any Work Executed by him.

FURNITURE.

Has the Largest Assortment of every description of

HOUSEHOLD FURNITURE.

Has the Best Selected Stock of

CARPETS. FLOORCLOTHS. MATS. AND MATTING.

BELSHAM

Has the Largest Assortment of

BRASS AND IRON BEDSTEADS.

Has the Cheapest

FENDERS AND FIREIRONS AND GENERAL FURNISHING IRONMONGERY.

Has the Cheapest

PAPER-HANGINGS.

FURNISHES HOUSES COMPLETE, The Cheapest

At any distance, CARRIAGE FREE.

Takes any kind of

FURNITURE IN EXCHANGE,

And BUYS FURNITURE to any amount.

A PERAMBULATORS.

The Cheapest

SECOND - HAND FURNITURE.

SO IF YOU WANT TO FURNISH A HOUSE, GO TO BELSHAM'S,

MOULSHAM-STREET, CHELMSFORD.

S. TWEED & SON,

WHOLESALE WINE AND SPIRIT MERCHANTS,

EPPING.

S. TWEED & SON are desirous of calling attention to the PRICE LIST appended below, and beg to state that the WINES and SPIRITS therein referred to have been selected with care and an earnest desire to place in the hands of their customers the best and purest that can be obtained in the field of competition. Their Bottled Port Wines have all been bottled and matured in their own cellars, therefore they offer them in confident hope of giving satisfaction.

Universally recognised as the one accurate Almanac and Handbook in the County.

JUST PUBLISHED,

In Crown 8vo, Price 6d., Limp Cloth 1s., Cloth Boards 1s. 6d. (by Post 8d., 1s. 2d., & 1s. 8d.)

THE

ESSEX ALMANAC & COUNTY HANDBOOK

FOR THE YEAR OF OUR LORD

1873—TENTH YEAR.

With a Variety of interesting and HITHERTO UNPUBLISHED Local and General Information.

TO BE HAD OF ALL BOOKSELLERS.

Every Saturday, of any Bookseller or News-agent, Price THREEPENCE.

Each Half-yearly Volume complete in itself with Title-Page and Index.

THE ATHENÆUM

JOURNAL OF ENGLISH AND FOREIGN LITERATURE, SCIENCE, THE FINE ARTS, MUSIC, AND THE DRAMA.

CONTAINS :—Reviews of every important New Book, English and Foreign, and of every new English Novel—Reports of the Learned Societies—Authentic Accounts of Scientific Expeditions—Criticisms on Art, Music, and the Drama—Foreign Correspondence on Subjects relating to Literature, Science, and Art—Biographical Notices of Distinguished Men—Original Poems and Papers — Weekly Gossip.

THE ATHENÆUM is so conducted that the reader, however distant, is, in respect to literature Science, the Fine Arts, Music, and the Drama, on an equality in point of information with the best-informed circles of the Metropolis.

With THE ATHENÆUM for December 28, a Special Extra Sheet will be issued, containing a series of articles on the Literature of France, Germany, Belgium, Denmark, Sweden, Norway, Holland, Hungary, Servia and Illyria, Italy, Portugal, Russia, and Spain.

*** No additional Charge will be made for this Double Number. A Single Copy will be sent upon receipt of Four Penny Stamps.

Published by JOHN FRANCIS, 20 WELLINGTON-STREET, STRAND, LONDON, W.C.

MALDON IRON WORKS COMPANY, LIMITED.

Directors.

Mr. J. BARRITT	...	Guy's, Maldon.	Mr. J. C. FLOAT	...	Maldon.
Mr. C. J. CARTER	...	Beek Hall, Little Totham.	Mr. A. G. SADD	...	Maldon.
Mr. H. FOSTER	...	Great Totham.	Mr. T. WORRAKER	...	Maldon.

Bankers.

Messrs. SPARROW, TUFNELL, PARKER, AND Co., Maldon.

Manager.

Mr. J. C. FLOAT.

THIS Company has been formed for the purpose of carrying on the BUSINESS of the late Mr. JOSEPH WARREN, Ironfounder and Manufacturer of Agricultural Implements, of Maldon.

The Directors respectfully solicit a continuance of the patronage and recommendation which has for many years been so liberally conferred on their late predecessor; while on their part they undertake that prompt and strict attention shall be given to the execution of all orders with which they may be favoured.

The transfer of the business to the Company will be made on the 31st instant, after which date all communications are to be addressed to the Manager, Mr. J. C. FLOAT.

Maldon, 12th December, 1872.

Figure 2. Part of the front page of the *Chelmsford Chronicle*, 3rd January, 1873.

BRIGHTLINGSEA PARISH MAGAZINE. 1

J. ALDOUS,

ACHT AND HOUSE DECORATOR,

Paperhanger, &c.

PECIAL attention is called to our preparation for Oil Clothes as we warrant it not to stick.

All kinds of Oil Clothes Cleaned off and Redressed.

BEARD & SON,

eneral and Furnishing Ironmongers,

2, ST. JOHN'S ST., COLCHESTER.

ottage and Leamington Ranges Tile Register Stoves, Marble and Enamelled Slate Chimney Pieces, Tile Hearths, Brass Fenders and Curbs.

PIPES & GUTTERS, CABLE CHAINS & ANCHORS.

COOPER COOPER & Co.

Sell the finest Tea the World produces at **2/10** a pound.

COOPER COOPER & Co.

Sell very choice Tea at **2/4** a pound.

COOPER COOPER & Co.

Sell a very special Black Tea of extraordinary merit at **2/-** a pound.

COOPER COOPER & Co.

Sell real Teas—sound, strong, true, and flavoury, at **1/8** and **1/10** a pound.

GENT—

WILLIAM PANNELL,

SUPPLY STORES, BRIGHTLINGSEA.

OND'S For Everybody

tent CARS. 12, 13 & 14, North Hill, Colchester.

ren's Carriages & Mail Carts. Paperhangings Wholesale & Retail

SPRING, 1894.

THOS. R. MILLS,

HIGH STREET,

Brightlingsea.

Has now a large and assorted

STOCK OF OUTFITTING

Fronts, Ties, &c.		6½d.
Noted Cloth Caps...from	1/- to	4/6
Black Felt Hats ...	„ 2/6 to	4/6
Socks, Handkerchiefs, and Braces......	„ 6½d. to	1/6
Boys' Knicker Suits	„ 2/11 to	10/6
„ Trouser Suits	„ 7/6 to	25/-
Men's ditto	„ 21/- to	30/-
Fashionable Jacket and Vest	„ 20/- to	30/-

Good Choice of NEW PATTERNS of Trouserings from 12/6, Suitings from 35/-

Good Fit & Style guaranteed.

ESTABLISHED, 1857.

SIGGERS & SON,

JOB & POST MASTERS,

AND

Funeral Carriage Proprietors,

SIR ISAAC'S WALK,

HEAD STREET,

COLCHESTER.

FUNERALS FURNISHED—

With Washington, Victoria, and Child's Cars, Hearses, Mourning Coaches, and Shillibeers.

Stylish and Up-to-Date Four-in-Hand BRAKES, BUSSES, &c.

LANDAUS, WAGGONETTES & HANSOMS.

Single or Pair-horse BROUGHAMS for WEDDINGS.

Lessons given in Riding and Driving.

A TRIAL SOLICITED.

Figure 3. Advertisements from *Brightlingsea Magazine,* 1894.

study of transport history including tramroads, docks, coastal shipping and turnpikes as well as railways and canals. Within such societies there is wealth of information on the many people and businesses connected with their subject. Examples of published information from the indexes of the Journal of the Railway and Canal Historical Society are articles entitled *Horncastle Navigation Engineers* in Issue xxv and *Personalities* in Issues xxiv and xxiii.

Business Bibliographies and Yearbooks

Many libraries and some County Record Offices will have many of the reference books of business & company bibliographies and company archives listed in the *Further Reading* chapter of this booklet. In addition major reference libraries, such as the City of London Business Library or the British Library Business Information Service, will have other finding aids for businesses. These will include the Stock Exchange Official Year Book which has been published since 1876 and the Stock Exchange cumulative Register of Defunct (Quoted) Companies which was last published in 1990 but in 1980 included some 23,000 companies.

3. *Locating Surviving Records*

National Register of Archives

Having discovered the names of companies and organisations which may be of interest, the starting point to find out what, if any, records have survived and are accessible, is the National Register of Archives (N.R.A.). This is located at the Royal Commission on Historical Manuscripts premises at Quality Court in off Chancery Lane, London near the Public Record Office (PRO). This organisation has compiled and maintains an index of over 23,000 companies whose records have been deposited. The Index is in a computerised database which may be accessed at a computer terminal in the public search room.

The Index may be searched under the following five headings and may be searched on any one of the five items.

1. Name
2. Type of Business
3. City/Town/Parish of location
4. County
5. Dates of deposited records

Illustrated is a printout of the last of three pages listing the companies located at Reading, Berkshire (*see figure 4*). Note that the information on a company in the Index contains brief details of the records deposited and the repository in which they are located. There is also a cross reference to an N.R.A. Acquisition Report from one of more than 1500 repositories contributing to the N.R.A. and this report, which is available on the open shelves, includes a detailed account of the records deposited. Where the repository is described as 'Private' as in the cases of J & C Simonds & Co. and Stephens, Blandy, Barnett, Butler & Co. of the example, reference to the N.R.A. Acquisition Report 23504 shows that the records are held by the Business Archives Council. This brief extract also illustrates the value of using the N.R.A. for locating archives as some

```
                    N.R.A. COMPANIES INDEX
                    ----------------------

   Simmons & Lawrence, estate agents, Reading, Berkshire
       c1840-1925: records
            Accessions to repositories 1985.  Berks RO

   H & G Simonds Ltd, brewers and maltsters, Reading, Berkshire
       1771-1976: corporate, accounting, sales, production, staff,
       premises and misc records
            Richmond & Turton, The brewing industry 1990.  Private
       1814-1971: minutes, share records, accounts, ledgers, journals,
       cash books, stock, brewing, staff and property records
            Richmond & Turton, The brewing industry 1990.  Greater
            London RO   ✗
       1891-1967: minutes etc
            NRA 31535 Courage.  Multiple Locations

   J & C Simonds & Co, bank, Reading, Berkshire
       1791-1933: partnership, customer, branch, investment and staff
       records, corresp and accounts
            NRA 23504 Banking survey.  Private

   Stephens, Blandy, Barnett, Butler & Co, bank, Reading, Berkshire
       1791-1899: partnership, customer, investment and premises
       records, corresp and routine accounts
            NRA 23504 Banking survey.  Private

   Suttons Seeds Ltd, seed merchants, Reading, Berkshire
       c1832-1970: partnership records, sales agreements, patent
       records, accounts, stock summaries, salaries and wages books,
       corresp
            NRA 20993 Suttons.  Inst of Agric History, Reading Univ


              ***  END OF LISTING  ***
```

Figure 4. Final page of a list of surviving records of companies located in Reading, *National Regiser of Archives.*

staff records, so useful to the family historian, of H & G Simonds Ltd had been deposited out of the locality in which the company was based at the Greater London Record Office.

If you are unable to make a personal visit to the search room, N.R.A. staff will answer specific limited enquiries by post.

Companies House
The business you are interested in may have been either a private or public registered company in England and Wales, which under the Companies Acts from 1844 had to be registered, and it is always worth searching Companies House indexes. These will indicate whether any

of the records of the administrative regulation relating to owners, directors and shareholders are held by Companies House or the Public Record Office. The word 'registered' is stressed because sole (or individual) traders, partnerships and some other companies, where the financial liability of running the company was not limited by the issue of significant numbers of transferable shares, were not required to register under succeeding Companies Acts. In the Public Search Rooms at Companies House, 55-71, City Rd, London (near Old St Underground station) and the branch offices elsewhere, there is an index on a computerised database for companies and their successors still in business now or dissolved in the last 20 years.

Nearly 70,000 companies were registered between 1856 and 1900 and a further 1.1 million in the years to 1976.

The question of of whether a company was required to register and it's status as a public, private or exempt private company is beyond the scope of this booklet but is dealt with more fully in the articles and PRO Information leaflet listed later under 'Further Reading'.

Do not discount companies still in business today. Many were begun in the 19th century or took over existing companies and information is held relating to their incorporation.

When using these indexes, and the card index mentioned later, it is important to realise that if any forenames or initials precede surnames in the leading part of the company title then you need to search on these. So, for instance, if you were searching for a company with the title commencing with E.D.PROBERT you need to search on 'E D' but if the title commenced with Eric D. PROBERT you would need to search on 'Eric D'.

For companies in existence in the 19th Century the most likely source is the extensive alphabetical card indexes to companies dissolved before 1964 or which changed name prior to 1975. These indexes used to be in the Public Search Room in London but are now located at Companies House at Cardiff and accessed only by the staff there.

Information on the card includes the company registration number, the date of dissolution and, if any administration records have been preserved, the Public Record Office box reference number. Files have been retained for all dissolved public and private non-exempt companies dissolved but only the files of 1% of the private companies exempt from filing annual returns dissolved after 1960 (reduced to 0.5% in 1977) have been preserved. The index cards for companies whose file has not been preserved are stamped 'Destroyed by arrangement with the PRO'. A Chelmsford company featured in the index, Aviation Transport Sales and Service Ltd, dissolved in 1956 and the records destroyed on 9th April 1964. Fortunately there is an index card for National Flying Services Ltd which was known to be involved in the 1930's with Aviation Transport Sales and Service Ltd. The Registration Number of the company, which was dissolved in 1958, is 238737 and the card is stamped 'File retained: passed to the PRO on 10/2/1964 Box 33076'. The 'Box' number refers to the location of the documents in the Public Record Office Class BT31, Files of Dissolved Companies, stored at Kew.

Information from the card index at Cardiff may be acquired either by sending a written request to Archive Searches, Room G.16, Companies House, CARDIFF CF4 3UZ or, provided that information is sought on only a few companies, telephoning this section on 0222 380928. Alternatively a simple form may be completed when at The Companies House Public Search Rooms in London, on which the name(s) of the companies of interest are listed. This form is then sent by facsimile (FAX) to Cardiff and, if the form is completed by 3.00pm then a reply on the same form is received by FAX in London the following working day. A search should be requested in both the dissolved company card index and the change of name index in case a successor company had been registered. The same service may be obtained from the branch offices in Manchester, Birmingham and Leeds.

If the company or name in which you are interested was not found in either card index then the computerised database may be accessed by the public from one of a bank of terminals in the search room. To see if the company was registered, the 'name page' of the database is accessed. It is necessary to select one of 3 options.

(*a*) Companies which are live or have been dissolved in the last 3 years.

(*b*) Companies dissolved in the last 20 years.

(*c*) Former Names Index relating to changes in the last 20 years.

After selection the name of the business is entered. However it is necessary to know at least the leading characters or words of the full title as the computer will list on the terminal screen all the company names which commence with the word or words that you have entered. For instance if you were interested to know if there were any companies registered with the name commencing with the surname PROBERT in the title you would just type in 'PROBERT'.

In fact searching on 'PROBERT' yields the following entries in the order listed.

> PROBERT (Builders) Ltd
> PROBERT(Fuels) Ltd
> PROBERT Haulage (Pontllanfraith) Ltd
> P ROBERTS & Co. Ltd
> PROBERT Software Ltd
> PROBERTS Printers Ltd
> PROBERTS Properties (Watling St) Ltd
> PROBERTS Self Service (1963) Ltd
> PROBERT Woollard & Partners Ltd

This example emphasises that the precise initial part of the name of the company is required for the search, as this search on PROBERT has also resulted in the surnmes ROBERTS and WOOLLARD being listed. Hence it is not possible to obtain a listing of all the companies having a given surname as part of the name.

All the information on registered companies is filed under the registration number which is listed on the 'Name' page and by entering this number into the 'General' page the following additional information is obtained.

> Date of Incorporation (Registration)
> Type of Company eg. Private Limited
> Whether Dissolved
> Date of Liquidation
> Date of last Annual Accounts Filed
> Date of last full Members (Shareholders) List

A further page, the 'history' page, can be accessed at a current cost of £1.00 per company and this gives the address of the registered office and lists the most recently filed documents for the company. However, the address may also be obtained from Kelly's Business Directory to be found in major reference libraries.

Guildhall (Corporation of London) Library

This library contains a number of Indexes and information which duplicates and in some cases adds to the information available from the Companies House card indexes but is directly accessible to the Public and useful as a cross-check.

1. An alphabetical strip index on microfiche of English and Welsh companies registered from 1856 to 1973, compiled from the following sources which are available in the Library.

(a) Joint Stock Returns–1856 to 1900

(b) Investors Guardian–1900 to 1962

(c) Jordans Daily Register–1963 to 1973

The listing includes the Company Name, Company Registration Number, Year of Registration, Source Document and page number.
As an example the entry for the company, Aviation Transport Services Ltd, referred to in the section on Companies House reads, 'Aviation Transport Services Ltd 407984 1946 A 127.

2. A microfilmed 'Change of Name' Card Index giving the same information as the Dissolved Companies Index and the new name.

3. A further card Index on microfiche listing companies dissolved from 1945 to 1973 which featured in the publication 'Stubbs Gazette' copies of which are held in the Library. This Index also includes companies registered in Scotland and Ireland.

4. A five volume alphabetical list of companies dissolved from 1856 to 1930. (48 hrs notice is required for the production of these documents as they are not stored within the Reading Room Building.)

5. The London Gazette Index of Partnership Dissolutions, 1785 to 1891. There is a cumulative index to 1811 but after this year it is necessary to search the indexes in the volumes for each year. To give some idea of the scope of this source, in 1811 over 1,800 dissolved partnerships and more than 4,500 bankruptcies were listed. Forty years later in 1851, over a 6 month period , there were nearly 1,400 partnership dissolutions but under 1,000 bankruptcies. A typical entry of a partnership dissolution in the *London Gazette* of 12 February 1811 (page 302) reads as follows.

Notice is hereby given that the partnership subsisting between Jane Parkinson, Annis Parkinson, Elizabeth Parkinson, Ellen Parkinson and

Maria Parkinson, all of Manchester in the County of Lancaster, milliners, under the firm of Jane Parkinson and Sisters was disolved by mutual consent on 31st December last. Witness their Hands this 26th day of January 1811.

The bankruptcies listed do of course include many individual bankruptcies as well as those of businesses.

6. Prospectuses of Companies seeking a quotation on the Stock Exchange. Those from 1824 to 1881 are bound alphabetically but thereafter to 1963 they are bound annually. The years 1824 to 1901 are available on microfiche.

Public Record Office (PRO), Kew

Registered Companies

It should be remembered that the records held in the PRO relate only to the administrative regulation of dissolved companies from incorporation to dissolution.

Class BT31 consists of the files of companies dissolved or re-registered after 1860 arranged by company registration number. This number may be obtained from the indexes at Companies House, Cardiff, the Guildhall Library or the following three printed alphabetical indexes at the PRO.

(a) Companies Registered from 1856 to 1920

(b) Companies in existence at 30th June 1930

(c) Companies in existence at 30th June 1937

Class BT41 comprises the files for over 4,100 general companies and just over 1,500 railway companies dissolved or re-registered before 1860, arranged alphabetically in two separate sections.

Class BT58 contains the correspondence files from 1871 of the Board of Trade, Companies Department, relating to approximately 3000 companies and organisations. Family history information is limited and appears to be confined to the original incorporation and subscribers. However as the class list contains an alphabetical index of company names it is a simple matter to check whether a file of any companies of interest to you is held.

Class BT95 comprises a single sheet of information for each exempt private company dissolved prior to 1944. However these are of little value to the family historian as they do not contain personal names and are arranged in order of date of incorporation, not company registration number or name, and only list the documents in the file that were destroyed at dissolution. A sheet will provide the basic information of company name, registration number, type & place of business and the dates of incorporation and dissolution.

Partnerships and Sole Traders

Unincorporated businesses were not registered until the Register of Business Names was established in 1916, later to be abolished in 1981. The Register was originally intended as a record of enemy aliens or former aliens not trading under their own names. Then it served as a register of persons or firms trading under a business name other than their own and persons or bodies trading under their own names were not required to register.

Class BT253 records only include the name, nature of the business, address and name of the Proprietor(s). Moreover, only a sample of the registrations in the years 1916/17 and every 10th year from from 1921 have been preserved. There are nearly 110,000 records of registration for the initial year but only 20,000 for 1931. The records are arranged in ascending order of Registration Number but The London Chamber of Commerce Library holds a microfiche index to business names cross-referenced to registration number and will answer specific enquiries by post and telephone.

Public Record Office (Chancery Lane)

There are some 19,000 files relating to companies that have had some dealing with the High Court of Justice in Class J13 and there is an alphabetical card index for the period 1891 to 1932 on open access in the Long Room. For the period 1923 to 1948 files are in the class list under their initial letter but from 1949 onwards only a representative selection have been preserved. As will be seen from the examples later in the booklet, the amount of family history information in the files is limited but as the material is indexed it is worth spending the few minutes necessary to search the indexes for the names of any companies of interest.

County Record Offices

Always search the Indexes, Guides, Handbooks and Catalogues for records of businesses, traders and partnerships that have been deposited. Do not neglect deposits by firms of solicitors who frequently acted as trustees and provided a secretarial service for businesses, public bodies, charities and agents for insurance companies, building societies and similar organisations. Records of their clients may also have been deposited.

Many business records are also to be found under the heading of Family and Estate papers, so these too need to be searched to see whether any have survived for the name or location of interest to you.

Company Archives

This book published in 1986 details the results of a survey of the records of 1000 of the first registered companies in England & Wales which were still on the Companies Register in 1980. It includes information on 674 companies and associated concerns whose records have been preserved and catalogued. All these companies were first registered between 1856 and 1889 but constitute about 4% of the total of the 30,000 plus companies registered in this 33 year period, the remainder having been dissolved.

The information comprises the company name, company registration number, address, a brief summary of the activities and history of the company including any changes of name and a list of the surviving records together with their location. The list is indexed by company name, location and subject.

As an example of the information available in the book, the listing for the Press Association Ltd indicates that office salary books for the period 1870 to 1968 are archived at their head office. There are 40 companies listed for the Bristol area and, for instance, the Theatre Royal, Bath holds records of the Subscribers (shareholders) to the Bath Theatre Royal Company for the period 1807 to 1847 in its archives.

4. Major Repositories: Examples of Records available

Business Archives Council

The Council is located in London and maintains a unique library of books and pamphlets on business history, many of which are privately published and not available elsewhere. There are currently over 4,500 publications in the library indexed by author, title and subject. The library may be used by members of the public if an advance booking is made but a Research Adviser will also deal with specific written enquiries on the existence of sources of information on particular businesses.

There are normally many references to employees, directors and others connected with the business in books on the history of a company and it is well worth searching the index for personal names. Depicted is an extract from the index of a book on the history of Courtaulds of Essex which shows just how many names may be mentioned (*see figure 5*).

Here are just a few titles picked at random from the shelves which illustrate the wide variety of material available of use to family historians.

Business History Journal, an article on the amalgamation of
   Corporate International Banks, 1855 to 1875.
The Peninsular & Oriental Steam Navigation Co. Ltd.
Scottish Industrial History Journal, an article entitled: *Records
   relevant to Scottish Industrial and Labour History in the Modern
   Records Centre,* University of Warwick.
Savills, A Family & Firm–1652 to 1977.
Dictionary of Business Biography, Vols 1 to 5, over 1000 biographies
   of British Business Leaders from 1860.
Shipping, A Survey of Historical Records.

INDEX 279

Figure 5. An extract from the index of *Courtaulds–An Economic and Social History,* 1969, showing many personal names.

History of the Union Bank of Scotland.
Accounting Business & Financial History Periodical, articles
   entitled *Fyffes and the Banana Centenary History, 1888 to 1988*
   and *Studies in the Business History of Bristol.*

County Record Offices

Here are some examples of deposited records, found in several record offices, which depict the variety of information that may be found including some records relating to small traders, shopkeepers and farmers.

Firstly from the Essex Record Office, the Dispensary Register of a Saffron Walden Chemist from 1897 to 1937 (D/F 15/1). Extracts from just two pages of several hundred in the Register are depicted (*see figure 6*). How else would you have known that Mrs Ingle of Radwinter was feeling depressed and taking a tranquilliser in December 1910 or that A. Hevish Esq. of the High Street was constipated?

In similar vein are the records of a surgeon, William Gaskoin Stutter of Wickhambrook, Suffolk, spanning seventy years from 1816 to 1887 in the form of a Prescription Book, Patient Ledger and Day Books of a Veterinary Surgeon from 1890 to 1918 deposited at the Bury St. Edmunds Branch of the Suffolk Record Office.

In the archives of the Hereford and Worcester Record Office are the shoemaking records of the Edwards family of Brampton Bryan, Herefordshire, including a record with names and details of the orders placed for shoes in the period 1916 to 1918.

Domestic and farming accounts for the 18th to 20th century of the Read family of Wembley are deposited in the Greater London Record Office.

Illustrated is a page from a book of funerals arranged in the period 1885 to 1901 by a firm of undertakers, Lewis of Stroud, Gloucestershire (D 2079/V/1) which is in the Gloucester Record Office (*see figure 7*).

The William Salt Library of the Staffordshire Archives Service has the accounts of customer's orders for the period 1775 to 1804 of John Poyser, a Yoxall grocer.

Documents such as these are well worth a search if the person of interest lived in the area and period for which records exist.

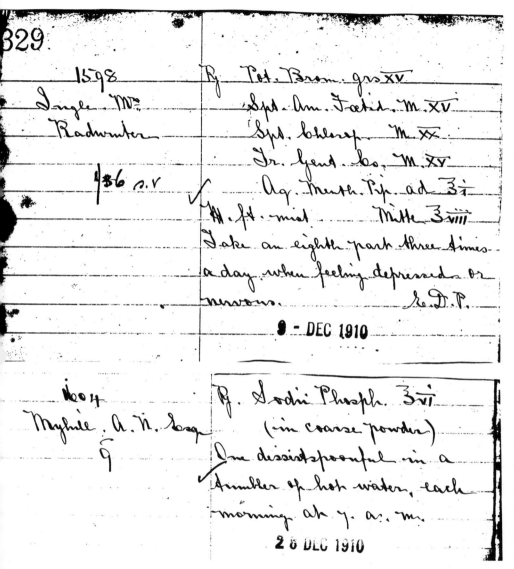

Figure 6. A Saffron Walden Chemist's Dispensary Register, 1897-1937, extract is for December 1910.

Sep. 27th 1895.

Funeral of the late
Mr Thomas Phipp
of the Parklands, Ruiscross
To be interred at Lainox Church
on Tuesday Oct. 1st 1895. at 2.30.

Officiating Clergyman
Revd E. W. Place B.A.

Sexton. Mr Geo. Chandler.
Coffin-maker. Mr E. Ashmead.

Bearers:-
Mr Wm Phipp.
   Stonehill Farm Nr Stroud
Mr Wm Phipps. Holcombe —
Mr Richd Hill Colwell Farm
Mr Geo. Chandler Rodboro'.

Mourners & Friends.

Mr S. Phipp	Nailop
— J. Phipp	Lanley Farm
— D. Phipp	Arlington
— P. Phipp	Dr Bell Pancross
— W. Hill	Stonehouse
— J. Hill	Stroud
— J. Hill	Cheltenham
— H. Holmes	Stonehouse
— a. Pinbury	Birmingham
— J. Pinbury	"
— E. Wathen	Stroud
— S. Butcher	Highfield
— E. Barnard	Eblet
— J. Merrett	Arlington
— W. Knee	Of Mr Walton Street Priest
— C. Curtis	Ruiscross
— W. Gastrin	"
— J. Phipp	Pin-comb Farm
— P. Witchill	Leonchurch
— E. Mablett	Leonchurch

Figure 7. An entry in the 'Book of funerals arranged 1885-1901' from undertakers *Lewis* of Stroud. The entry is for September 1895.

A considerable amount of documentation on the activities of the many Building Societies has survived and from The Saffron Walden Building Society in Essex is an extract from the Subscription Book of 1860 to 1867 (Essex R.O. D/F 34/13) which lists persons subscribing for shares (*see figure 8*). Note the mention of family relationships, places of residence and occupations. Also deposited is a Minute Book for the years 1849 to 1867 which lists Officers of the Society including the Chairman, Vice Chairman, Directors and Auditors. The minutes also feature the names of those to whom mortgages were advanced and the interest payable. Another example of Building Society documentation that has survived are the Investors ledgers from 1856 to 1927 of the Leek and Moorlands Permanent Benefit Building Society to be found in the Stafford County Record Office.

Many records of Public Utilities, such as Water, Gas and Electricity suppliers, have survived and from the Hereford and Worcester Record Office is an extract from the pages of an 1840 to 1853 Cash Book (C98/1) for the Hereford to Gloucester Canal Company (*see figure 9*). This details the names of and payments for the many activities of the suppliers of goods and services to the Company. The author's interest in this extract is of course in the William Probert who was supplying brash, loose broken rock, for the new wharf at Ledbury.

Records of many businesses have been deposited with Birmingham Central Library, Archives Division. For instance 19th Century wages books (MS 1010/8) of Ralf Heaton & Sons, coin, wire and metal tube manufacturers, are available which give a weekly alphabetical listing of wages paid to employees. In July 1841 there were 21 employees, including five women, and payments ranged from 2s 1d to Jane BROWN to £3 2s 8d for Thomas ODHAMS. By 1861 there were 145 employees listed, sometimes with their trades noted with the lowest paid employee, Sarah BARDELL, earning 2s 8d whilst several workers on piecework were earning wages between £10 and £15 per week. Also in these archives is a 1770's receipt book for a canal carrier, Thomas Jackson & Co., (MS 1067) and the 19th century day books of a varnish, japan & colour manufacturer, Meredith & Co., established in 1780. Illustrated is one page from the book covering the years 1827 to 1871 (MS 1068/1)

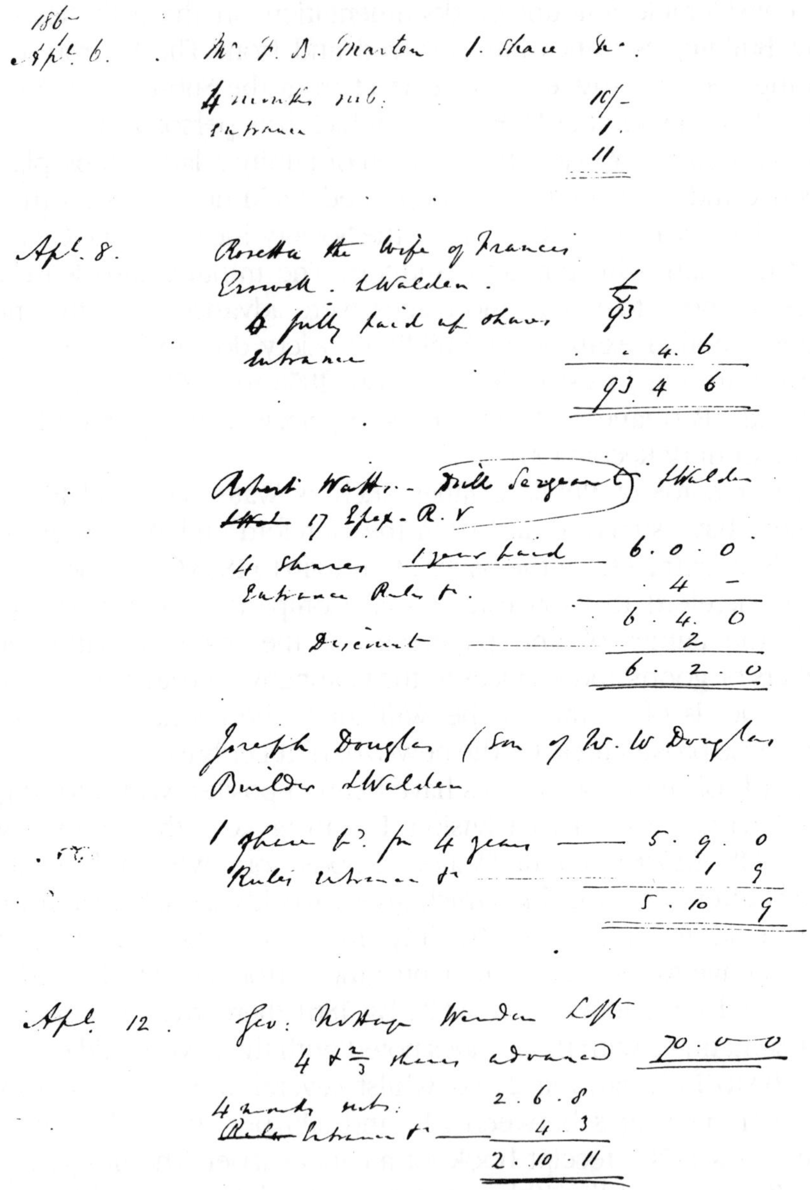
186-
Apl. 6. Mr. F. A. Marten 1. Share &c.
4 months sub: 10/-
Entrance 1.
11

Apl. 8. Rosetta the Wife of Francis
Errwell. S. Walden.
6 fully paid up shares £ 93
Entrance . . 4. 6
93. 4 6

Robert Watts – Drill Sergeant of S. Walden
17 Essex R.V.
4 Shares 1 year paid 6. 0. 0
Entrance Rules &c. . 4 -
6. 4. 0
Discount 2
6. 2. 0

Joseph Douglas (Son of W. W. Douglas
Builder S. Walden
1 Share pd. for 4 years 5. 9. 0
Rules entrance &c 1 9
5. 10 9

Apl. 12. Geo: Northrop Wenden Lofts
4 & 2/3 shares advanced 70. 0 0
4 months subs: 2. 6. 8
Rules entrance &c 4. 3
2. 10. 11

Figure 8. A subsription book of *Saffron Walden Building Society*, 1860-1870.

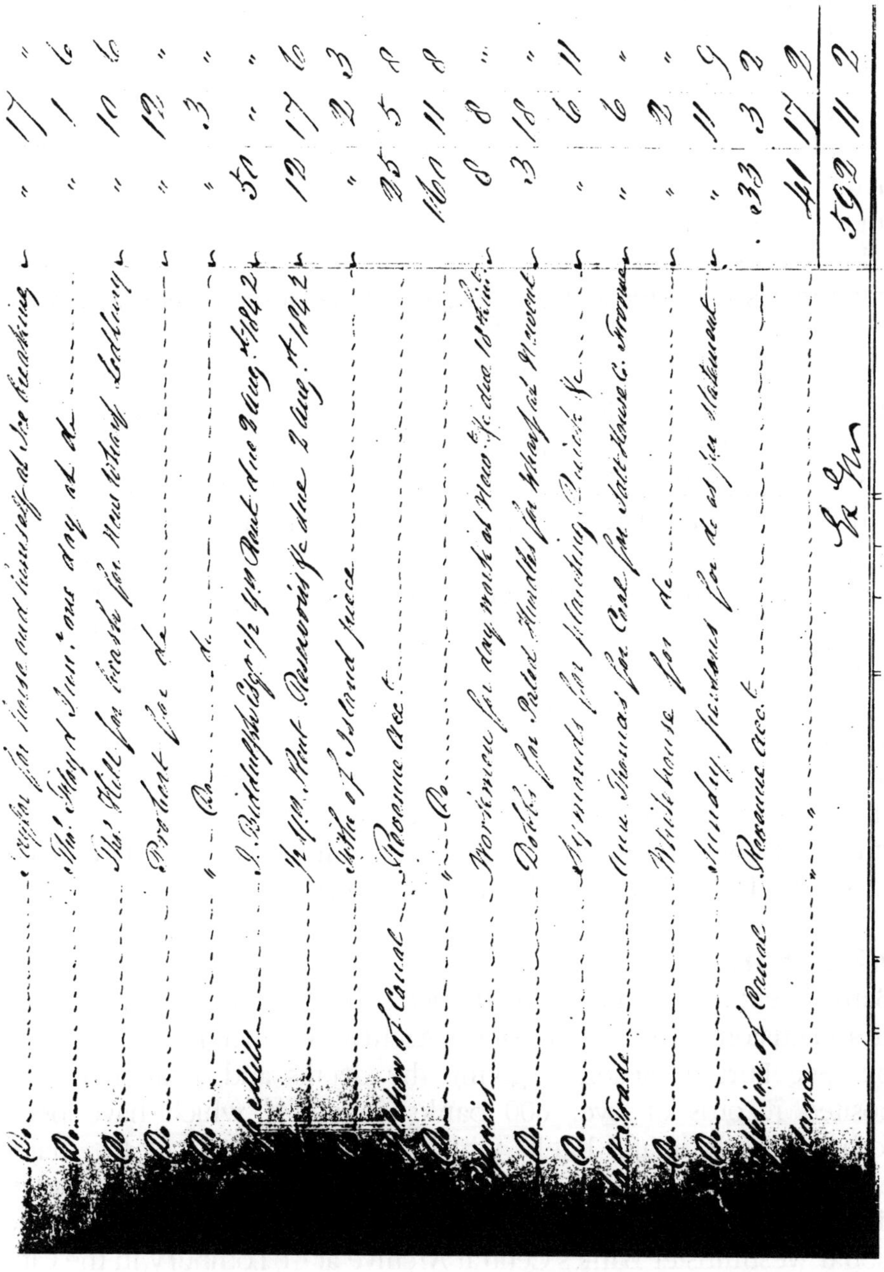

Figure 9. Extract of a page from a cash book, *Hereford and Gloucester Canal*, 1840-1853.

recording the supply of materials to customers around the country (*see figure 10*).

In the Essex Record Office there is an outstanding collection of documents dating back to the early 19th century deposited by Samuel Courtauld and Company, silk manufacturers of Essex. The documents contain remarkably detailed information on employees, especially women, and their families. Presented here are exampless of just a few of the documents available.

Firstly there is a register with an index of all the women employed in the Finishing Department of the Bocking Factory from 1860 to 1908 (D/F3/2/22) Depicted are a few extracts giving information on family relationships and character (*see figure 11*). Then there is a Register of all those women who applied for employment from 1864 to 1892 (Ref. D/F3/2/24). The page illustrated gives an indication of the valuable family history information (*see figure 12*). For the Halstead factory there is an alphabetical Register of employees for the period 1873 to 1899 complete with their employment history. The depicted extract for George Bower of Bradford (*see figure 13*) shows just how much detail was recorded especially concerning previous employment.

It may not be generally known that in compliance with Factory Acts dating from as early as 1833, employers were required to record details of all workers under the age of 18 years in an official register. One for the years 1836 to 1844 has survived but is to fragile for photocopying to be permitted. However a double page from a similar register for the later year of 1912 (D/F3/5/6) is reproduced (*see figure 14*).

Bank Archives

Banks seem to have a particularly rich source of information on both staff and customers and the Business Archives Council has published a book (See Further Reading) giving the details and location of the deposited records of over 600 banks, many of which have been absorbed into the major banks which exist today. Most of the major banks have archives to which limited access to the public is given and in which staff will deal with specific written enquiries. As an example the National Westminster Bank's Central Archive at 41, Lothbury in the City of London near the Bank of England holds a wealth of records from

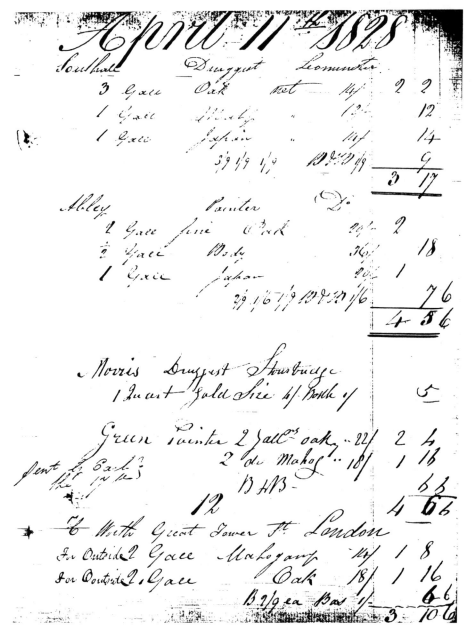

Figure 10. Page from the Day Book, *Meredith and Company,*
Birmingham, 1827-71.

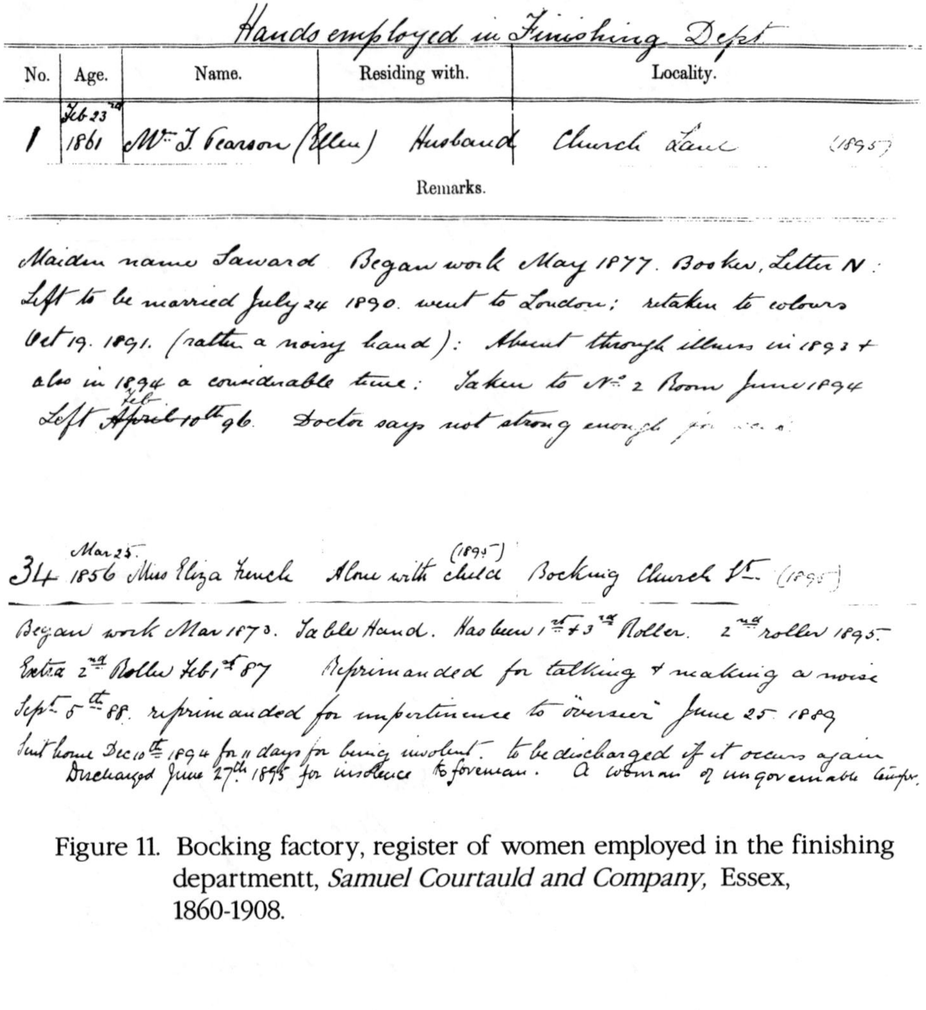

Hands employed in Finishing Dept.

No.	Age.	Name.	Residing with.	Locality.
1	Feb 23rd 1861	Mrs J Pearson (Ellen)	Husband	Church Lane (1895)

Remarks.

Maiden name Saward. Began work May 1877. Booker, Letter N. Left to be married July 24 1890. went to London; retaken to colours Oct 19. 1891. (rather a noisy hand): Absent through illness in 1893 + also in 1894 a considerable time: Taken to No 2 Room June 1894 Left April 10th 96. Doctor says not strong enough for ...

34 | Mar 25. 1856 | Miss Eliza French | Alone with child (1894) | Bocking Church St. (1895)

Began work Mar 1870. Table Hand. Has been 1st + 3rd Roller. 2nd roller 1895. Extra 2nd Roller Feb 1st 87. Reprimanded for talking + making a noise Sept 5th 88. reprimanded for impertinence to overseer June 25 1889 Sent home Dec 10th 1894 for 11 days for being insolent. to be discharged if it occurs again Discharged June 27th 1895 for insolence to foreman. A woman of ungovernable temper.

Figure 11. Bocking factory, register of women employed in the finishing departmentt, *Samuel Courtauld and Company,* Essex, 1860-1908.

Figure 12.   Extract from a register of applications by women for employment at the Bocking Factory, *Samuel Courtauld and Company*, Essex, 1860-1908.

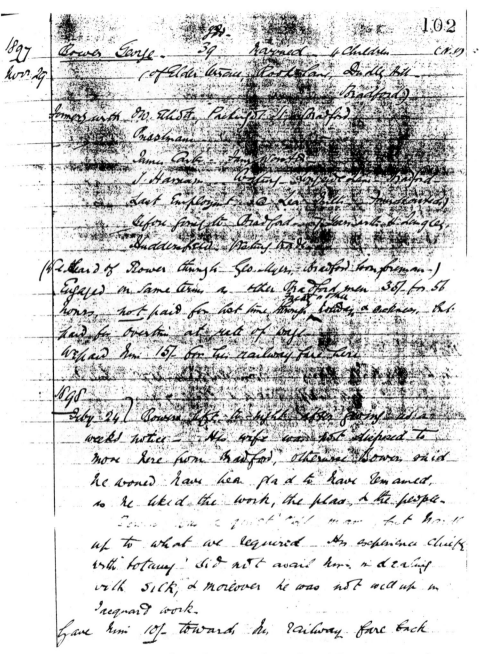

Figure 13. Register of employees at the Halstead Factory, *Samuel Courtauld and Company,* Essex 1873-1899.

head office and Branches of this bank and many others that have been taken over.

Some examples of surviving records from the former London and County Bank serve to illustrate the variety of source material and extent of the information available.

Firstly with regard to staff there is a series of registers of employees of the bank at head office and the branches from 1868 to 1908. Within the registers the branches appear alphabetically year by year and as you can see from the example from Chelmsford Branch in 1868, (*see figure 15*), the information given on transfers enables an employee's career within the bank to be traced.

In addition there is a run of the bank's house journal, the 'County Magazine' from 1907 which includes obituaries and staff changes.

Information on customers may be found in at least the following four types of documentation.

1. *Signature Books,* dating from the mid-18th Century, which were used to record the opening of an account and details of the account holder including address and occupation. During the 19th and early 20th Century it was mainly professional, tradespeople, shopkeepers and farmers who were opening bank accounts but there was also a sprinkling of more humbler folk. This is shown on a double page from the book for Chelmsford in 1885 (*see figure 16*).

2. *Information or Character Books* which were written up either when the account was opened or possibly when a loan was required and provide biographical information on the account holder and sometimes family relationships. This text from the Information Book of the Brentford Branch for 1887 on a High St. Jeweller, Thomas Pearce, is typical. An old a/c opened 13/9/72 & respectfully conducted. Mr. Pearce has a good business his wife holds 3 L&C Shares Mr Pearce's name is also on the share register joined with B. Reid but this is money belonging to B. Reid alone Mr Pearce is well known to Mr. Jas Gray. unsecured. Another from the book of the South Kensington Branch in London in 1879 illustrates that an indication of family relationships and status may be found. 14th May 1879, Banks Penelope, Spinster Lady of 134, Queens Gate, SW Introduced by her Mother who banks at < blank > Branch of

rt II. YOUNG PERSONS.

Register of Young Persons (under 18 years of age) employed Full Time, and

See Instructions on page ii. of cover.

TO BE FILLED IN BY THE OCCUPIER.

Columns 2, 3, 4 and 5 to be filled in before the Young Person is allowed to commence work.

Surname.	Christian Name.	Residence.	Date of First Employment.	In case of persons between 13 and 14 years of age. Date of Labour Certificate from Local School Authority, qualifying for full-time Employment.
(2)	(3)	(4)	(5)	(6)
Pluck	Gladys May	East St Braintree	July 15 1912	2nd April 1912
Shelley	Esther	Buckwood Cottages Rd. Notley	July 25 1912	22nd July 1912
May Allen	Rhoda Emma Louise	13 Allens Road Braintree	July 26 1912	14th December 1911
Allen	Helen May	Coggeshall Road Braintree	July 29 1912	
	W			
Clark	Beatrice	107 East St Braintree	Aug 12 1912	April 15 1912
Butcher	Lily	Fairfield Street Braintree	Aug 15 1912	April 11th 1912
Sayers	Constance Ethel May	4 Bradford Street Bocking	Aug 9 1912	
Lines	Minnie Ethel	80 Bois St Braintree	Sept 14 1912	
May	Eva Loy	24 Church St Braintree	Sept 23 1912	
Newman	Florence Winifred & Ethel	52 East St Braintree	Oct 8th 1912	Dept.
Norman		107 Bocking Road, Braintree	Oct 8th 1912	
Shead	Ethel	Mill Hill Braintree	Oct 14 1912	Oct 10. 1912
Richardson	Florence Ann	14 Bois St Braintree	Oct 28th 1912	May 3rd 1912
Saunders	Gladys	40 Notley Rd Braintree	Oct 30 1912	
Starey	Florence Edith	Buckwood Cottage Notley Road Nov 11 1912		Oct 31st 1912
Green	Beatrice Ellen	124 Church St Braintree	Nov 4 1912	
Willer	Ellen Dorothy	Buffs Lane Rd Notley	Nov 6 1912	Sept 2 1912

(P21)

(14094)

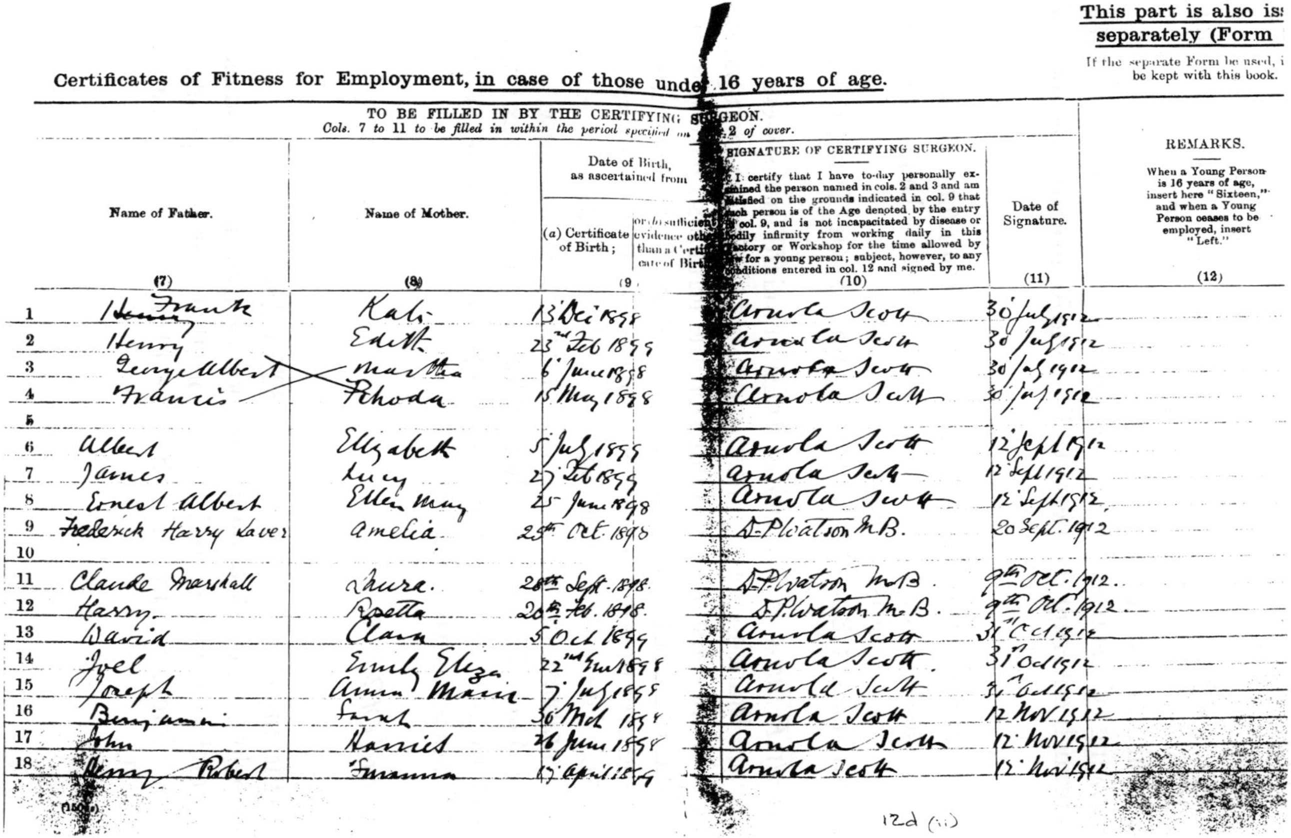

Figure 14. Register of Employment of Young Persons, *Samuel Courtauld and Company*, Essex, 1912.

L & C Bank, and then in another hand, married June 1892 to Mr. I. Anderson.

3. *Safe Custody Registers* recorded customers deposit and withdrawal of documents such as share certificates, deeds and valuable goods such as silverware & jewelry. Columns in the register include the date, name of depositor, description of the item, where deposited in the bank, date of withdrawal and withrawer's signature.

The following two entries taken from year 1875 of the Register of the Hertford Branch covering the period 1859 to 1876 give an indication of the information which may be found.

Date	Acc. Name	Security	Location	Withdrawal & Sig.
13 Mar	H.Lanaway	Ins. Policy & Russian Bond	Small Safe	13 Nov Hugh Lanaway
11 Jul	Cath Masters	Box of Plate	Strong Rm	20 Aug James Foster

4. *Quarterly Returns of Overdrafts.* These standard forms were completed by each Branch every quarter and listed the name, occupation and address of the Customer. Columns on the form also gave the ammount of the overdraft, a description and value of any security, the amount of the overdraft in the previous quarter and if the overdraft was sanctioned the date and amount together with the Manager's remarks upon the desirability or otherwise of continuing the advance. As an example, the March 1872 quarterly Return for the Halstead, Essex Branch recorded many people including a bankrupt, coal merchant, surgeon, brewer, solicitor and several farmers.

Public Record Office, Kew

Class BT 31

E.H.Smith (Birmingham) Ltd (PRO: BT 31/32761/214718)

The file includes the following information on this family business of builder's merchants, factors and contractors that was incorporated as E.H.Smith & Company Ltd on 24th June 1926 with the registration number 214718.

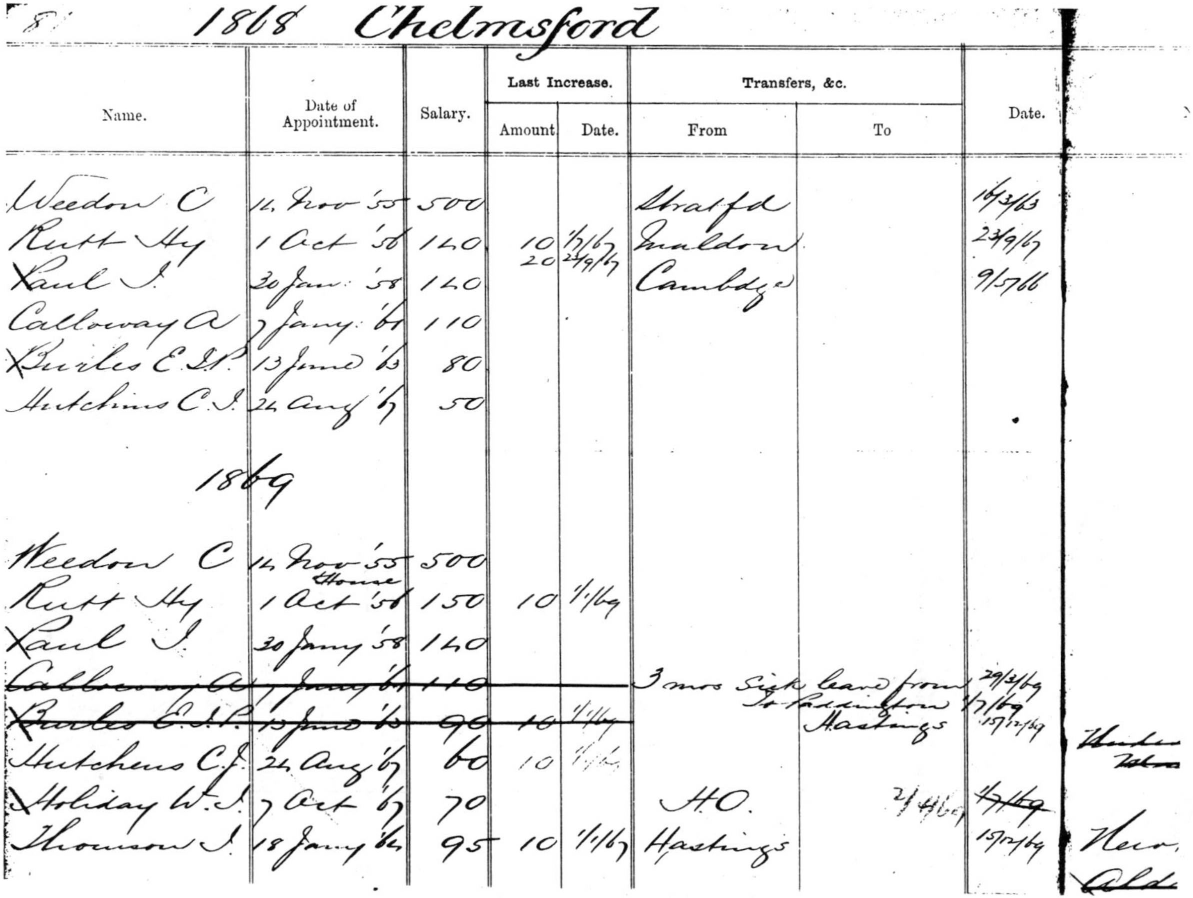

1868 Chelmsford

Name.	Date of Appointment.	Salary.	Last Increase. Amount	Last Increase. Date.	Transfers, &c. From	Transfers, &c. To	Date.
Weedon C	14 Nov '55	500			Stratfd		16/3/63
Rutt Hy	1 Oct '56	140	10 20	1/1/67 24/9/67	Maldon		23/9/67
Paul J.	30 Jan '58	140			Cambdge		9/5/66
Calloway A	7 Jany '61	110					
Burles E.J.P.	13 June '63	80					
Hutchins C.J.	24 Aug '67	50					

1869

Name.	Date of Appointment.	Salary.	Last Increase. Amount	Last Increase. Date.	Transfers, &c. From	Transfers, &c. To	Date.
Weedon C	14 Nov '55	500					
Rutt Hy	1 Oct '56 House	150	10	1/1/69			
Paul J.	30 Jany '58	140					
~~Calloway A~~	~~7 Jany '61~~	~~110~~			3 mos sick leave from		29/3/69
~~Burles E.J.P.~~	~~13 June '63~~	~~90~~	~~10~~	~~1/1/69~~		To Paddington	1/7/69
Hutchens C.J.	24 Aug '67	60	10	1/1/69		Hastings	15/12/69
Holiday W.J.	7 Oct '67	70			H.O.	2/4/69	~~1/7/69~~
Thomson J.	18 Jany '64	95	10	1/1/67	Hastings		15/12/69

Figure 15. Register of Officers at Head Office and Branches, *London & County Banking Co.*, Chelmsford, 1868-9.

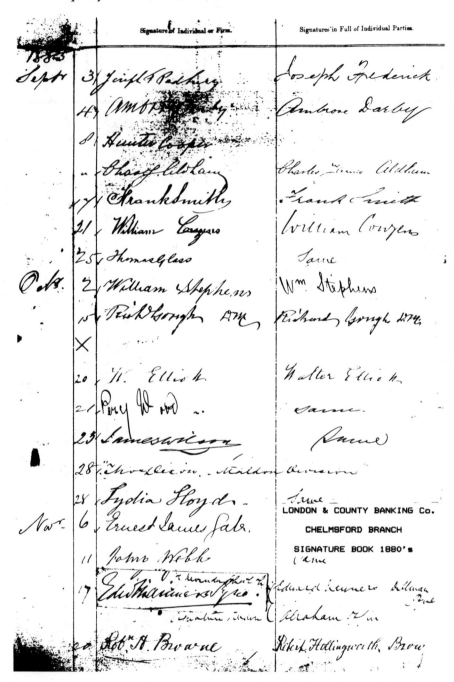

Figure 16. Two pages from the Signature Book of the Chelmsford Branch, Essex, *London & County Banking Co.,* 1880s.

168

Name & Address	Business or [Profession]	By whom Introduced
Albert Place, New London Road, Chelmsford	R.C. Priest	Hackney?
11 Moulsham St	[illegible]	[illegible]
30 Moulsham	Hay & Straw dealer	Brentwood
Aythrop Roding, [illegible]	Retired Photographer	Son of [illegible]
Wells & Sheds Farm, Roxwell	Farmer	
Kings Arms Inn, Moulsham Street, Chelmsford	Publican	Brentwood
Temple Farm, West Hanningfield, Chelmsford	[illegible]	
Mark Hall, Margaret Roding, Dunmow	" 5.5[?]	G. Millbank
[illegible] Villa, [illegible] End, Chelmsford	Drill Master	[illegible]
Greatstone Stock, The Common	Retired Estate Gentleman	[illegible]
[illegible] Witham	Farm Steward	Known
Springfield	[illegible] to R. Wilson	deed
Chelmsford	[illegible]	[illegible]
21 Duke St Chelmsford	Wife of Richard [illegible]	[illegible]
Orslands, Bradwell on Sea, Southminster	Farmer, Hollywell Farm	Known
Whittle	Farm Bailiff	[illegible]
Roveden Rectory	Clerk in Holy orders	
do	Farmer	
Willows St, Baddow, Nr Chelmsford	Out of Business	[illegible]

1. Memorandum and Articles of Association in which the initial
    Subscribers are listed as:
    *Ernest Howard Smith, Merchant, of 59, Broad Grn Rd, Acocks Grn,
    B'ham.*
    Charles Smith, Builder of 265, Stratford Rd, B'ham and whose
    signatures were witnessed by:
    Edna May Smith, Clerk of 265, Stratford Rd.
2. Certificate of Incorporation.
3. Directors' particulars.
4. Change of registered office.
5. Summary of share capital & shares, 1927.
6. Change of Name Certificate.
7. Annual Return for 1936 detailing the following shareholdings
    Ernest Howard Smith Director of 44, Flint Green Rd, Acocks Grn.
    1,200 ordinary shares, 200 transfered to *E.M. Smith Fredeline
    M. Smith, Director of 44, Flint Green Rd, Acocks Grn.*
    100 ordinary shares
    Edna May Smith, Secretary of 31, Malvern Rd, Acocks Grn.
    200 ordinary shares
    Mary Amelia Smith } *Administrators of C. Smith, deceased*
    Ernest Howard Smith
    *Westhaven Investment Trust Ltd, 1, Market Place, Ashby de la
    Zouch*
    500 ordinary shares, 2,000 deferred shares
8. Liquidator's Statement of Account, 18 May 1938.
9. List of Dividends paid to Creditors, 18 May 1938.
10. Return of final Winding Up Meeting, 18 Apr 1939, showing details
    of realisations from debtors, disbursements to creditors and
    repayment of capital.
11. Affidavit verifying statement of Liquidator's account showing
    all disbursements including some to Westhaven Investment Trust
    Co. Ltd, Storey & Smith Ltd and E.H. Smith (Westhaven) Ltd.

You can see that the above includes a considerable amount of
information concerning this family, together with names of other
companies in which the family were involved where further searches
may be fruitful.

Crosville Motor Company (PRO: BT 31/17897/90577)

The documents on file for this Chester company provide evidence of a small business incorporated in 1906 with only 7 Subscribers but by 1926 there had been considerable expansion as the Annual Returns list, with names, addresses and number of shares held, approximately 600 shareholders. The company was wound up in 1929.

Class BT 41

Chelmsford Corn Exchange Company (PRO: BT 41/137/795)

The Memorandum of Association of this company states that it was incorporated on 16 May 1857 to erect and provide the necessary buildings and accommodation in Tindal Square, Chelmsford for a Corn Exchange and Auction Rooms and other rooms suitable for public and private use. A page from the Memorandum document includes the signatures, places of residence and number of shares held by the Initial Subscribers (*see figure 17*). A year later, the Annual Return for the company includes an alphabetical listing of the considerable number of shareholders together with their place of residence and occupations. The first page of this list is reproduced (*see figure 18*) and includes the name of 'Frederic Chancellor', the architect who built the Corn Exchange.

West of England & Forest of Dean Coal Co. (PRO: BT 41/744/4013)

This company was incorporated on 17th Nov 1852 with the object of 'working the coal fields of the Forest of Dean in the County of Gloucester for sale by various lines of railways and otherwise'. What is particularly interesting is that although the company was promoted by a local man, Henry Young of Ruradean, the Head Office was in London at 15, St Saviours Yard, London Bridge and the five Directors on 25th July 1854 all lived in the London area. The Directors were:

Frederick Henry Fitzharding Berkeley of 1, Victoria Square, Pimlico
John Yates, Secretary to the Eastern Steam Navigation Co.,London
Thomas R. Vermont Esquire of Hayes, Mddx
James Russell, coal merchant of Belmont Wharf, Kings Cross, Mddx
    residing in Croydon
George Butcher, coal merchant of Belmont Wharf, Kings Cross, Mddx
    residing at 2, Upper Vernon St, Lloyd Square, Pentonville, Mddx.

WE, the several persons whose Names and Addresses are subscribed, are desirous of being formed into a Company, in pursuance of this memorandum of Association, and we respectively agree to take the number of Shares in the Capital of the Company set opposite our respective names.

Names and Addresses of Subscribers.	No. of Shares taken by each Subscriber.
Edmund Brund Springfield *Essex*	(50) Fifty
James Beddel Broomfield *Essex*	(25) Twenty five
W.? Wells Chelmsford *Essex*	Fifty
Thos D Ridley Chelmsford *Essex*	Ten (10)
William Brown Broomfield	Five
Henry Marriage Broomfield *Essex*	Five
James Christy ? Roxwell *Essex*	Five
Wm Seabrook Boreham *Essex*	Five
Job Murphy Jepp Chelmsford *Essex*	Ten

Figure 17. Memorandum of Association giving details of Initial subscribers subscribers, *Chelmsford Corn Exchange Company*, Essex, 1853.

List of Persons holding Shares in the *Chelmsford Corn*
on the *Twenty fifth* day of *June 1858*—, and of Persons
Year immediately preceding the said *Twenty fifth* —— day
Addresses, and an Account of the Shares so held.

Folio in Register Ledger, containing Particulars.	NAMES, ADDRESSES, AND OCCUPATIONS.			
	Surname.	Christian Name.	Address.	Occupation.
1	Bradel	James	Broomfield Lodge Essex	Estate Agent
2	Bramston	Thomas William	Skreens Roxwell Essex	Esquire
2	Bygrave	John Joseph	Woodham Walter Essex	Gentleman
2 & 3	Bradel	William James	Brentwood Essex	Estate agent
3	Baker	Robert	Writtle Essex	Estate agent
3	Bell Bell and Smith	Mary James Joseph John	Woodham Walter Essex 103 Devonshire Place portland place middlesex Ockleigh Essex	widow Esquire Farmer
3	Bintall	Edward Hammond	Heybridge Essex	Ironfounder
3	Bridge	Thomas	Prittlebury Essex	Farmer
3 & 4	Christie	William	Chelsea Middlesex	Miller
4	Crush	William	Chignal St James Essex	Farmer
4	Christy	James the younger	Boynton Hall Roxwell Essex	Farmer
4 & 5	Chancellor	Frederic	Chelmsford Essex	Architect
5	Christy	James	Broomfield Essex	Farmer
5	Disney	Edgar	The Hyde Ingatestone Essex	Esquire
5 & 6	Duffield	William Thomas	Chelmsford Essex	Solicitor
6	Durrant	Andrew	Chelmsford Essex	Innkeeper
6	Durrant	Thomas	Bocking Essex	Innkeeper
6	Duffield	James	Great Baddow Essex	Farmer
6	Ely	John	Great Leighs Essex	Farmer
6	Foster	Joseph	Witham Essex	Farmer
7	Gepp	Thomas Morgan	Chelmsford Essex	Solicitor
7	Hutley	William	Witham Essex	Farmer
7	Isaac	Thomas	Maldon Essex	Corn merchant
7	Josling	William	Great Waltham Essex	Farmer

Figure 18. Extract from a list of shareholders from the annual return of the
Chelmsford Corn Exchange Company, Essex, 1858

Class BT 58

Two examples of records for organisations in these files of correspondence of the Companies Dept of the Board of Trade illustrate the information held.

1. *Women's Aerial League of the British Empire* (PRO: BT 58/31 COS 1387/1909).

The file relates to correspondence concerning the ommission of the word 'Limited' from the title of the organisation which was registered in June 1909. However, included with the correspondence is the Memorandum of Association and this yields the names, addresses, occupations and, in three cases, family relationships of the original Subscribers. There are some famous ladies amongst these Subscribers *(see figure 19)*!

2. *Catholic National Insurance Trust Ltd* (PRO: BT 58/108 COS 1915/1927). This file also includes a copy of the Memorandum of Association listing information on the seven Roman Catholic Clergy who were Subscribers in 1927.

Class BT 253

Includes the standard forms completed by sole traders and partnerships when registering their business. Depicted is an example of the form completed for a business entitled Annette which demonstrates the limited information included (*see figure 20 *).

In addition there were forms for notifying changes to the business or its partners which can provide valuable family history information. For instance, Certificate No. 107262 (PRO: BT 253/0355) yielded the information that one of the partners, Edwin Gibson, of the Crewe Arms Motor Co. had died on 25th Jan 1926 and that the company was transformed into a private limited company as from January 1927. Even more valuable was the information on Cert. No. 189877, dated 15 March 1917, relating to Charles Holland & Co., a house, estate and insurance agency in West Ealing, which advised that one partner Thomas George Yoell of Langley was now Private 189877 in the Motor Transport Division of the Army Service Corps in France whilst the other, Norman White, late of 23, Milverton St, Leomington, Warwickshire, was now with the 10th Middlesex Regiment in India. Unfortunately it is pure chance to find such information as there is no index to partners names.

16

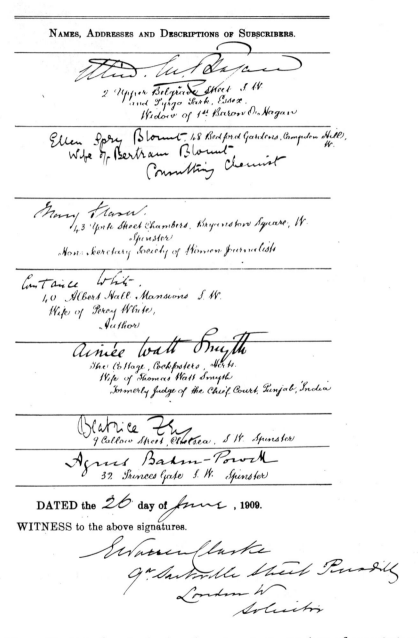

Figure 19. List of orginal subscribers to a memorandum of association *Women's Aerial Leage of the British Empire,* 1909.

20 JUL 1931

A 5/- adhesive stamp must be affixed in the space provided.

The Statement must be sent or delivered in
England and Wales to The Registrar of Business Names, North East Wing, S...
House, London,
Scotland to   do.   do.   Exchequer Chambers, Par...
Square, Edinburgh.

GREAT

2 0 JUL 1931

Form R.B.N. 1a.

No. of Certificate.

REGISTRATION OF BUSINESS NAMES ACT, 1916.

314892

Application for Registration by a Firm.   See Sec. 1 (a) and (c).

Insert name of Firm,   *ANNETTE*   , hereby apply for
registration under the provisions of the Registration of Business Names Act, 1916,
and for that purpose furnish the following statement of particulars :—

1. The business name.	*ANNETTE*
2. The general nature of the business.	*General Drapery*
3. The principal place of the business.	*5 The Broadway, Shenfield Essex*
4. The date of the commencement of the business, if the business was commenced after 22nd Dec., 1916.	*10 - 7 - 31*
5. Any other business name or names under which the business is carried on.	

(Y6247)   Wt 9679/5900   12,000   9/30   H & Sr   Gp 108
(Y6955)   Wt 20288/6016   12,000   8/31

55

[P.T.O.

Figure 20. The Forms of Registration for *Annette*, a general drapery business
of Shenfield, Essex, 1931.

		1	2	3
See Note B at back	6. The present Christian name or names, and surname, of every individual who is— and the corporate name of every corporation which is— a partner in the firm.	MRS ~~ANNA~~ ANNIE. DUKE.	MRS. ELSIE. MARY. GREGSON	
See Note C at back	7. Any former Christian name or names or surname of every individual partner in the firm.	—	—	
	8. The nationality of every individual partner in the firm.	British	British	
	9. The nationality of origin (if other than the present nationality) of every individual partner in the firm.	—	—	
	10. The usual residence of every individual who is— and the registered or principal office of every corporation which is—a partner in the firm.	Dunbar. Cromwell Rd Stanfield.	BRAEMAR. LAKE AVENUE. BILLERICAY	
	11. The other business occupation (if any) of every individual partner in the firm.	—	—	

Dated the __16.__ day of __July__ 19 3 1.

Signatures

Annie Duke

Elsie Mary Gregson

Public Record Office, Chancery Lane

Class J 13

These records arise from actions heard in the Companies Court of the High Court of Justice under the Companies (Winding up) Act 1890 and subsequent legislation, and they include orders, petitions and judge's notes. The following are just a few examples of the information that can be found from the files.

Southey Bros, Hosiers of Brick Lane, London in voluntary liquidation (Case 0042 of 1911, PRO: J 13/6048)
The names and addresses of the solicitor and liquidator are given as well as the names of creditors. A brief history of the business is stated together with the names of the principal shareholders, William John Southey & Miss Olivia Southey and George Paynter & Mrs Alice Paynter.

A.G. Mumford Ltd of Colchester, Essex in voluntary liquidation. (Case 00614 of 1933, PRO: J 13/13590).

This file includes an application by a former employee, Sales Manager William Abdy Sycamore of White lodge, Brightlingsea, Essex and includes an affidavit signed by him as well as information on the Managing Director of the company James Aitkin Kinnaird.

Thomas Tapling & Co. Ltd, carpet warehousemen and furniture & bedding manufacturers of Yiewsley, Middlesex
(Case 0062 of 1943, PRO: J 13/17564)

This file of the Judge's copy of a petition concerns a proposal to alter the objects of the Company within the Memorandum of Association and of particular interest to the family historian is the reference to those involved in the original incorporation of the Company in 1891. The first page of the petition includes this information (*see figure 21*) whilst later pages refer to the financial situation of the Company at that time and the names of the major shareholders.

IN THE HIGH COURT OF JUSTICE   No.*OO63* of 1943

CHANCERY DIVISION

MR. JUSTICE BENNETT

IN THE MATTER of THOMAS TAPLING & CO., LIMITED

                         - and -

IN THE MATTER of THE COMPANIES ACT, 1929.

TO HIS MAJESTY'S HIGH COURT OF JUSTICE

                         THE HUMBLE PETITION of THOMAS
                         TAPLING & CO., LIMITED,

SHEWETH as follows :-

1.   YOUR Petitioner the above-named Thomas Tapling & Co.,
Limited (hereinafter called "the Company") was incorporated
on the 24th day of August 1891 under the Companies Acts 1862
to 1890 as a Company limited by shares.

2.   THE Registered Office of the Company is situate at
Onslow Mills, Trout Road, Yiewsley in the County of
Middlesex.

3.   THE Objects for which the Company was incorporated
were:-

(a) To acquire the goodwill of the business carried on at
Gresham Street, and elsewhere, in the city of London and
in the county of Middlesex, under the style or firm of
"Thomas Tapling & Co." and to acquire and undertake the
whole of the assets and liabilities of the proprietors
of that business in connection therewith, and with a
view thereto to adopt and carry into effect an agreement
which has already been prepared, and is expressed to be
made between Victor Loraine Tapling of the first part,
George Smith of the second part, William Pheasant of the
third part, Alfred John Barton Tapling of the fourth
part, the said Victor Loraine Tapling, William Pheasant
and George Smith and Walter Yeates Hargreaves of the
fifth part and Thomas Parker Morgan of No.25 Cheapside,
in the city of London, warehouseman, on behalf of the
Company of the sixth part, a copy whereof is set forth
in the schedule to the Articles of Association of the
Company.

Figure 21. A petition to the Chancery Division of the High Court of Justice,
Thomas Tapling & Co. Limited, Yiewsly, Middlesex, 1943.

Guildhall (Corporation of London) Library

A Handlist of Business Archives at the Guildhall Library (See Further Reading) details the deposited records of over 800 businesses of individuals, tradesmen, partnerships and companies, mostly from the City of London. There is an alphabetical business name and subject listing, cross referenced to a more detailed card index catologue. Some records require at least 24 hours notice prior to production. A few examples of the wide ranging types of records are given below.

For Stratton & Gibson, Merchants trading with Russia, of 9, Gt St. Helens, City of London, there is an account book for the years 1804 to 1809 (MS 19,777 Vol. 2) which details in immaculate copperplate writing the insurance, commissions, bills receivable and interest payable to named individuals and retailers.

A register of items supplied by the watch and clock makers, Parkinson & Frodsham in the 19th Century from 1866 (MS 19,909) and indexed to 1873, gives the names and frequently the addresses of clients all over the World. A typical entry is that for August 1891 when Mr. D. Smith of 'The Limes', Ingatestone, Essex was supplied with pearl safety pins at a total cost of £1 2s 6d.

In particular, The Guildhall Library also holds the records of over 80 London based insurance companies which include the fire policy registers for the Hand-in-Hand Fire and Life Insurance Society from 1696 to 1865, the Sun Insurance Office, 1710 to 1863 and the Royal Exchange Assurance, 1773 to 1883. Most of the Hand-in-Hand policy registers have personal name indexes but only for their London area clients. The registers for the Sun and Royal Exchange include clients from all over Britain but there are only indexes for comparatively short periods of time (1775 to 1787 and {Sun only} 1714 to 1731). The surviving registers include a wealth of information for the family historian including the name, status and occupation of the policyholder and the location, type and value of the property insured, as well as the names, occupations and addresses of any tenants.

Companies House

If you have discovered a company of interest to you in the registered company computer database or microfilm listing, then copies of administrative documents for current companies and those dissolved in the last 20 years are available on microfiche. The packet of microfiche is ordered by the company registration number through the computer terminal. Payment at the rate of £3 per company is made by means of a plastic 'search card' purchased in the search room and inserted into a slot at the computer terminal.

In the London search room, the microfiche are then sent to a delivery point in a packet (*see figure 22*), normally within two hours of being ordered and may then be viewed on readers in the search room and, if required, photocopies may be made on self-service machines at a cost of 10p per frame. If you do not wish to wait for the packet to be delivered then you can have the packet posted to you for the payment of a further £2.50. Fiche of companies registered in Scotland may also be ordered from the London or provincial Offices. Should it not be convenient to visit the London search room, a postal service for the search, and supply of the microfiche packet for a company, if found, is available from the Companies House Cardiff Office at a cost of £5.50 per company. (Charges at the time of going to press).

There may be several fiche in a packet and the envelope for Humphries and Tapling, for example, contained 8 fiche.

The information given includes the key administrative documents for the company such as the Articles and Memorandum of Association, Appointment of Liquidator and the Liquidator or Receiver's statements of accounts as well as the accounts and annual returns for the last 3 years.

The fiche are letter coded and sequentially numbered in the chronological order in which the documents were filed. The 'A' coded fiche contains the annual returns and accounts, the 'M' fiche details charges or mortgages and liquidation (if any) whilst the 'G' fiche contains the incorporation documents.

Documents filed containing personal names include:
1. Lists of names and addresses of Directors at incorporation and new Directors appointed during the life of the company.
2. Allotments to shareholders (Members) with names and addresses at incorporation and changes during the life of the company.
3. List of Creditors for a liquidated company.

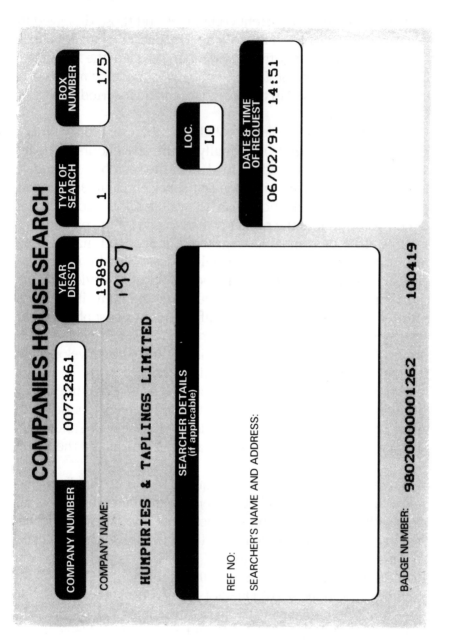

Figure 22.   The packet in which the fiche for *Humphries & Taplings Ltd.,* of Yiewsley, Middlesex, are presented in from Companies House.

Examples are shown from the administrative documents of the dissolved company, Humphries and Tapling, which went into liquidation on the 7th Nov 1986.

Lists of Creditors (*see figure 23*) show the amount owing to them and the amount of dividend paid in that year. Note entries for members of the Tapling family and the information on deceased creditors and the names of solicitors acting as their executors. One of the subsidiary companies of Thomas Tapling and Co. Ltd (featured earlier in this Section under PRO, Chancery Lane) was the Yiewsley Carpet Company and there were a number of documents relating to this company in the packet of fiche. As an example the share allotment for December 1950 is depicted (*see figure 24*), showing the amount of personal information included.

Specialist Archives

There are a number of Archives which hold records of businesses with references to personal names in a particular sector and listed below is a selection known to the author, which gives an indication of the wide scope of the information available (See chapter 6 for addresses and telephone numbers).

BBC Written Archives Centre. This centre holds around 100,000 files relating to speakers, writers, artists, composers and entertainers engaged by the BBC in both radio and television up to 1962. Most of the files contain copies of the contracts, details of programme participation and related correspon-dence. It also holds is an indexed collection of press cuttings of broadcasters from 1922 to 1962.

Institute of Agricultural History. This is in the Rural History Centre (formerly known as the Museum of English Rural Life) of the University of Reading. The Institute houses records of about 2,500 companies involved in farming, agricultural engineering, food processing & distribution and farm & garden seed production. There are extensive collections for a number of companies including Ransomes, International Harvester Co., Suttons Seeds and Rank Hovis Mc Dougall.

Modern Records Centre. This Archive, at the University of Warwick has an extensive collection of documents on Co-operative and Employer Associations.

Surname	Christian Name	Amount of Proof £	Amount of Dividend (or Composition)	
			Paid £	Unclaimed £
Sutton Upholstery		101.39	3.71	
Thomas Tapling Co.	Limited	1,932.62	70.70	
Tele Nova Limited		606.72	22.19	
Thames Water		78.50	2.86	
Style House (Bristol) Limited		124.35	4.54	
Tollit & Harvey Limited		120.57	4.41	
Trafford Carpets Limited		6,840.52	250.26	
Trotters Limited		9.97	35	
Laurence Turner Limited		118.23	4.32	
United Linen Services Limited		11.04	40	
N.B. Waite & Sons Limited		15.00	54	
Western British Road Services Limited		3,646.58	133.40	
E.A. Youdell		224.86	8.22	
Paul Zellers Discount Warehouse		262.52	9.61	
Coleman	P. (Mrs.)	30.00	1.09	
Docherty	J.G. (Mr.)	75.00	2.73	
Mayhew	C.N. (Mr.)	117.03	4.27	
Snelgrove	C.C. (Mr.)	53.81	1.96	
Alcock	G. (Mr.)	435.57	15.94	
Amor	H.G.N. (Mr.)	74.51	2.72	
Anderson	M. (Mrs.)	130.69	4.78	
Bailey	A.R. (Mr.)	292.29	10.68	
Branton	E.M. (Mrs.)	108.89	3.98	
Brooks	E.J. (Mrs.)	418.38	15.30	
Brook	A. The Hon. (Mrs.)	727.97	26.61	
Brooks	C.A. (Mr.)	401.19	14.68	
Brown	J.E. (Mr.)	74.51	2.72	
Coles	E.M. (Mrs.)	143.28	5.23	
Conen	H.W. (Mr.)	34.39	1.25	
Connor	G.P. (Mrs.)	143.28	5.23	
Cottlesloe G.B.E.	(The Lord)	10,161.51	371.76	
Craxford	W.J. (Mr.)	133.08	4.86	
Davies	G.I. (Miss)	34.39	1.25	
Drabble	W. (Mr.)	34.39	1.25	
Edwards	E.E. (Miss)	217.79	7.96	
Wilson & Wilson Solicitors, executors for (Mrs. G.M. Everard, deceased)		399.25	14.60	
Wilson & Wilson Solicitors, executors for (Mr. L.V. Everard, deceased)		544.47	19.91	
Everard	S. (Miss)	143.28	5.23	
Tapling	J. (Cmdr. The Hon.)	3,484.46	127.48	
Fyfe	M.P. (Ms.)	82.56	3.02	
Hadley	A.B. (Mr.)	143.28	5.24	
Hales	N. (Mrs.)	292.29	10.69	
Hall	G.H. (Mr.)	183.40	6.71	
Handy	A.L. (Mr.)	108.89	3.98	
Harding	K.M. (Mrs.)	510.08	18.66	
Hobson	E.E.	34.39	1.26	
Holloway	J. (Mrs.)	2,034.59	74.43	
Holmes	C.F.	34.39	1.26	
Honey	M.C. (Mr.)	57.31	2.10	
Hoyle	A.	2,361.27	86.38	
Hughes	L.M. (Mrs.)	510.08	18.66	
Total £		62,543.87	2,303.34	

Figure 23. List of creditors, *Humphries & Tapling Ltd.,*
Yiewsley, Middlesex, 1986.

Museum in Docklands. The Project Library and Archive of this Museum holds the staff records from the beginning of the 19th Century of a number of the private dock companies that operated along the River Thames and similar records for the Port of London Authority from the early 1900's.

National Archive of Electrical Science and Technology. This archive, maintained by the Institution of Electrical Engineers in London, includes the records of such companies as Laurance Scott Electromotors of Norwich (1883 to 1939) and J.A. Crabtree Ltd, manufacturers of domestic electrical equipment (1919 to 1939). It is also rich in the papers, biographies and obituaries of eminent electrical engineers and scientists.

National Maritime Museum. The Library of this Museum at Greenwich has an extensive collection of documents and books on companies involved in shipping, ship-building and marine insurance.

Post Office Archives. The Post Office has been one of the largest employers in the country and records of appointments survive from 1831 onwards. The search room is open to the public where there are personal names indexes, salary lists, appointments books and pensions records which enable careers of all staff from Postmaster to the humble letter carrier and messenger boy to be traced. Annual Establishment Books, complete with indexes, which date from 1742 and were printed from 1858 to 1959, detail the careers of all those employees entitled to a pension. An extract from a page of the Establishment Book of 1891 (*see figure 25*) features the entry for I. Probert, who filed a joint Patent Application described in the following 'Science Reference and Information Service', and traces his career in the Post Office for nearly 30 years.

The Archive also has a run of the former Post Office house journal entitled 'St. Martin's le Grand Magazine' from 1891 to 1933. These contain much biographical information on Post Office employees and have been indexed.

Names, Descriptions, and Addresses of the Allottees

SURNAME.	CHRISTIAN NAME.	ADDRESS.
BARNES	George Reginald	39, Woodland Way, Winchmore Hill, London, N.21.
DRABBLE	Walter	60, Swanage Waye, Hayes, Middx.
FREMANTLE	John (The Hon.)	32, Hampstead Grove, London, N.W.3.
HOLMES	Charles Frederick	59, Holmwood Road, Cheam, Surrey.
HOYLE	Alan	45, West Drayton Park Avenue, West Drayton, Middlesex.
HOYLE	Sydney	2 , Hillside Court, Finchley Road, London, N.W.3.
HYATT	Albert Robert	3, Kidbrooke Gardens, Blackheath, London, S.E.3.
THOMAS TAILING & CO., LIMITED		55-57, Leonard Street, London,E.C.2
-do-		-do-
BIDDLE	Lawrence Austin	)
BANKES	John Wynne	) Administrators of Eugene Vandenbroucke, deceased. 1, Gresham Street, London, E.C.2.
VANDORPE	Marcel	Rue du Phoenix 5, Mouscron, Belgium.
WOODS	Reginald	60, Ferrers Avenue, West Drayton, Middlesex.

Figure 24. Share allotment, *Yiewsley Carpet Company,* 1950.

DESCRIPTION.	½ Red. Cum. NUMBER OF SHARES ALLOTTED.		
	Preference.	Ordinary.	Other kinds.
Brought forward ...			
Company Director	22		
Works Engineer	24		
Company Director	123		
Departmental Buyer	24		
Company Director	24		
Company Director	133		
Departmental Buyer	24		
Warehousemen	7,801		
-do-	599		
Solicitors	265		
Constructeur	437		
Dyer	24		
Total	9,500		

Signature ....

Dated the fifth *day of* December 19 50

Officer .... Secretary.
(State whether Director or Secretary.)

Printing Archives. One of the Corporation of London libraries, The St. Bride Printing Library, has an extensive collection of historical documents covering the printing, papermaking, bookbinding, publishing, bookselling, news-paper & periodical and typefounding industries. The University of Reading Library also holds records of printing and publishing companies including The Bodley Head Ltd, Jonathon Cape Ltd, De La Rue & Co. Ltd and London Typographical Designers Ltd.

Science Reference and Information Service. This part of the British Library, located just off Chancery Lane in London, houses the records of British and Overseas patent applications and inventions. As well as yearly volumes of patent titles indexed both by company name and the personal name of the applicant, there is a set of of 284 microfiche which list the names of all people, companies and organisations associated with British Patent specifications from 1615 to 1980.

Having found a name of interest in the indexes, reference to the Patent through the patent number may well lead to the name of an employing organisation and address for the applicant. The extract from the first page from Patent Application Number 18,935 (*see figure 26*) made in 1895 for 'regulating electrical supplies' illustrates this point.

South Wales Miners Library. The Library of the University of Swansea houses some of the records of South Wales Miners' Institutes and the National Union of mineworkers, as well as of some collieries.

Archives of Existing Companies

Many of the larger companies have a reference library and employ an Archivist, at least on a part-time basis. Most allow limited access by the public to their records by prior appointment. A listing of some 80 existing companies, mostly those in Membership of the Business Archives Council (BAC), maintaining archives is contained in the 'Directory of Business Archives' published by the BAC (See Further Reading).

33

LONDON.

ENGINEER-IN-CHIEF'S OFFICE. (TELEGRAPHS).			
Date of Civil Service Certificate.	Dates of Appointments.	Name.	Salary.
		Submarine Superinten-dent (Woolwich). £500, increasing by £25 per annum to £700.	£ £
B.	E. T. Co., 8 Oct. 1853; G.P.O., 29 Jan. 1870.	Lumsden, D. - -	680
		Submarine Superinten-dent (Dover). £400, increasing by £20 per annum to £550.	
B.	E. T. Co., 14 Sept. 1869; G.P.O., 29 Jan. 1870; Asst. Submarine Super., Woolwich, 1 March · 1878 ; Submarine Super., Dover, 21 Aug. 1890.	Culley, W. R. - -	415
		Assistant Submarine Superintendent (Woolwich). £310, increasing by £15 per annum to £450.	
19 June 1890*	Late Submarine Tel. Co., G.P.O., 1 Apr. 1889; Asst. Submarine Super., Woolwich, 21 Aug. 1890.	Marsh, H. - -	310
		Assistant Submarine Superintendent (Dover). £250, increasing by £10 per annum to £350.	
C. 18 June 1885	E. in C.O., 8 Sept. 1873; Tel. T.S., 20 July 1885 ; Insp. E in C.O., 21 July 1885; Asst. Submarine Super., Dover, 21 Aug. 1890.	Pollard, F. - -	250
		Superintendent of Electric Lighting. £310, increasing by £15 per annum to £400.	
13 Feb. 1869 C.	E.T. Co., 29 Oct. 1864; Clk. Shrewsbury, 13 Feb. 1869; Asst. Super. School of Telegraphy, 31 July 1872 ; Super. of Electric Lighting, 17 Sept. 1889.	Probert, I. - - -	325

Messengers (2).

20s. per week, increasing by 1s. per week annually to 40s.

Boy Messengers (3).

Under 1 year - 8s.	Above 2 and under 3 years - 10s.
Above 1 and under 2 years 9s.	„ 3 years - - 12s.

B. Appointed under Telegraph Act, 1868.
C. Appointment legalized under the Superannuation Post Office and War Office Act, 1876.
* Certificated under Clause VII. of Order in Council of 4th June 1870.
A 64560.

C

Figure 25. Post Office Establishment Book, reference to I. Probert, 1891.

N° 18,935

A.D. 1895

Date of Application, 9th Oct., 1895

Complete Specification Left, 3rd July, 1896—Accepted, 8th Aug., 1896

PROVISIONAL SPECIFICATION.

Improvements in Apparatus Employed in Regulating Electro Motive Force in Alternating Current Circuits for Theatre Lighting or other Useful Purposes.

We, ISAAC PROBERT, of 25 Union Road, Clapham, in the County of Surrey, Electrical Engineer, and ERNEST FRANCIS MOY, of 20 Loraine Road, Holloway, in the County of London, Electrical Engineer, do hereby declare the nature of this invention to be as follows :—

Our invention relates to improvements in apparatus employed in regulating the electro motive force in alternating current circuits, for controlling the lighting of theatres, and for other useful purposes.

Figure 26. Patent Application No. 18,935, 1895-6.

Such archives normally comprise the following types of records.

1. *Personnel records*

Almost invariably the 100 year rule applies to these and sometimes there is no access at all. For instance one of the author's former employers, The Marconi Co Ltd which is now GEC-Marconi and has a part-time archivist, declined to provide a copy of the application the author made to join the Company in 1957. Apparently it was annotated with notes made by the interviewers!

2. *Employment Records*

Documents such as Wages Books & Staff Registers have sometimes survived and are normally made available. As an example the catologue of the private Cadbury archives shows that in addition to wages & salaries books, registers of directors, managers, employees, personnel with long service and apprentices have been preserved from the-mid 19th Century, some listed alphabetically.

The Cadbury Brothers Girls Office Wages Book for the 3rd quarter of of 1927 (Ref. 321/001972), for example, features an entry for the author's Mother, Winifred Buck, giving the dates of her employment and the amount of wages paid. An extract from a page of the similar, but earlier, Girls Office Wages Book No. 4 (Ref. 312/001884) which includes the employee's date of birth, dates of employment and, where applicable, the name and abode of the person she married *(see figure 27)*.

3. *Newspaper Cuttings*

These relate to the Company and the activities of it's employees and are normally filed in chronological order but seldom indexed.

4. *Biographies and Obituaries*

These are mainly for prominent company employees and are often filed in alphabetical order or indexed.

5. *House Magazines or Journals*

As pointed out elsewhere in this booklet these can be a rich source of information. For example, in a typical Issue of the 'The Marconi Companies and their People, the house magazine of the author's former employer, there are ten pages of photographs and information on the company's employees and their families. This information

NAME	Check Number		Folio		Department
Hodgkiss Emily	5048		117 ✓	241	Card Box
Hodgkiss Emaby	4054	4060	6 ✓	214	F Block Sugar
Hodgkiss Kate	4604		92	244	F Block Top
Hodgkiss Lizzie	3158				C Block Top
Hodgkiss Minnie	4304	4345	76/233	48	C Block Bott
Hodgkiss Sarah	4900		107		F Block Bott
Hogan Ethel	3169				C Block Top
Hoffman Edith E	424	4352	83	4 ✓	C Block Bott
Hoffman Ruth	4467	4352	234	232	C Block Bott

Figure 27. Extract from girl's register No. 4, *Cadbury Brothers Ltd.*

116

orn	Came	Left			Remarks
49	1·16·94	12·20·02	Good		Mar: W H Hall Cotteridge
84	5·29·00		Good		Mar: A Probert Northfield
8 84	11·2·94				
7·87	8·25·02				
82	6·25·95				
2·74	1·23·88	4·3·00	V Good		Married G Mann Cotta...
85	9·16·02				
78	9·25·94	12·21·00	Good		married W Ward Shirbley
84	1·28·01				

includes births, marriages, promotions, departures from the company, retirements and sporting achievements. You may even be very lucky and find a three generation family tree, complete with photographs as the extract from Volume 34 1944 'Co-Partners' Magazine', the journal of The Gas Light and Coke Company shows (see figure 28).

6. *Published Company Histories*

Many companies have published privately or commissioned the publication of books on their history, often to coincide with a centenary celebration of their founding. Some may still have copies available for sale.

ANOTHER FINE RECORD—*The Mercer Family*

The Mercer family can claim nearly 450 years of service with the Company, and with several members still on the pay roll the family may well pass the 500 mark. All have been at Beckton. The original William Mercer began work at Beckton in 1864, and retired as Carpenter Foreman after 40 years. His seven sons all entered the Company: William II, Robert, Charles, George, Thomas, Samuel and Frederick. William II served for 55 years before he retired, and one of his sons, Albert, is still with us as a Blacksmith. Charles has two sons, William and Alfred, to carry on their father's tradition. Charles himself retired as a Loco Driver after 50 years of service. This Company is very proud indeed of such families as the Mercers, and we are glad to publish photographs of some of its members.

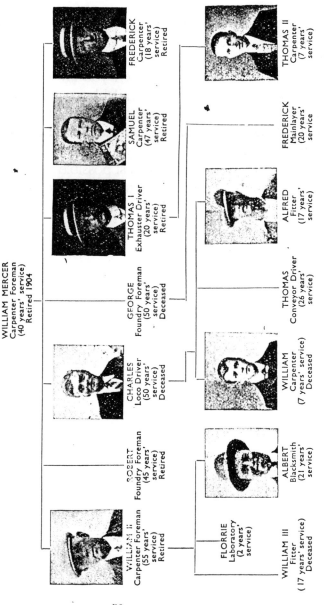

WILLIAM MERCER
Carpenter Foreman
(40 years' service)
Retired 1904

WILLIAM II
Carpenter Foreman
(55 years' service)
Retired

ROBERT
Foundry Foreman
(45 years' service)
Retired

CHARLES
Loco Driver
(50 years' service)
Deceased

GEORGE
Foundry Foreman
(50 years' service)
Deceased

THOMAS I
Exhauster Driver
(20 years' service)
Retired

SAMUEL
Carpenter
(47 years' service)
Retired

FREDERICK
Carpenter
(18 years' service)
Retired

FLORRIE
Laboratory
(2 years' service)

WILLIAM III
Fitter
(17 years' service)
Deceased

ALBERT
Blacksmith
(21 years' service)

WILLIAM
Carpenter
(7 years' service)
Deceased

THOMAS
Conveyor Driver
(26 years' service)

ALFRED
Fitter
(17 years' service)

FREDERICK
Mainlayer
(20 years' service)

THOMAS II
Carpenter
(7 years' service)

Figure 28.   The Mercer family tree published in *Co-Partners' Magazine*, *The Gas Light and Coke Company*, London, 1944.

73

5. Conclusion

It is hoped that the booklet has given you an insight into the rich variety of information that may be available on our ancestors in the surviving records of companies, businesses and similar organisations. Only a sample of the source material available has been presented but the object has been to encourage you to widen the search for information on your ancestors and suggest possible avenues for research. Hopefully too, guidance has been given on how and where to seek out this information. It is now up to you. Good luck with your searches!

6. *Useful Addresses and Telephone Numbers*

England & Wales

Archive of Art & Design
23, Blythe Rd, LONDON W14 0QF. Tel. 071 602 6907

BBC Written Archives Centre
Caversham Park, READING, Berks RG4 8TZ. Tel. 0734 472742

British Association for Local History
Shopwyke Manor Barn, CHICHESTER, West Sussex PO20 6BG. Tel. 0243 787639

British Library (The)
Business Information Service, 25, Southampton Buildings, LONDON WC2A 1AA. Tel. 071 323 7457

British Library (The)
Science Reference & Information Service, 25, Southampton Buildings, LONDON WC2A 1AW. Tel. 071 323 7472

British Library (The)
Newspaper Library, Colindale Ave., LONDON NW9 5HE. Tel. 071 323 7353

British Telecom Archives & Historical Information Centre
Room G09, Telephone House, 2-4, Temple Avenue, LONDON EC4Y 0HL. Tel. 071 822 1002

Business Archives Council
The Clove Building, 4, Maguire St, Butler's Wharf, LONDON SE1 2ND. Tel 071 407 6110

Companies House (Head Office)
Crown Way, CARDIFF CF4 3UZ. Tel. 0222 380801

Companies House (The London Search Rooms)
55-71, City Rd, LONDON EC1Y 1BB. Tel. 071 253 9393

Companies House (Manchester Branch)
75, Mosely St, MANCHESTER M2 2HR.   Tel. 061 236 7500

Companies House (Birmingham Branch)
Birmingham Central Library, Chamberlain Square, BIRMINGHAM B3 3HQ.   Tel 021 233 9047

Companies House (Leeds Branch), 25, Queen St, LEEDS LS1 2TW.   Tel. 0532 338338

Corporation of London Business Library
1, Brewers Hall Garden, LONDON EC2V 5BX.   Tel. 071 638 8215

Corporation of London Guildhall Library
Aldermanbury, LONDON EC2P 2EJ.   Tel. 071 332 1868

Corporation of London St. Bride Printing Library
Bride Lane, LONDON EC4Y 8EQ.   Tel. 071 353 4660

London Chamber of Commerce
69-75, Cannon St, LONDON EC4N 5AB.   Tel. 071 248 4444

Modern Records Centre
University of Warwick, W. Midlands CV4 7AL.   Tel. 0203 524219

Museum in Docklands
Project Library & Archive, Unit C14, Poplar Business Park, 10, Prestons Rd, LONDON E14 9RL.   Tel. 071 515 1162 & 071 538 0209

National Archive for Electrical Science and Technology
The Institution of Electrical Engineers, Savoy Place, LONDON WC2R 0BL.   Tel. 071 240 1871

National Maritime Museum
Romney Rd, Greenwich, LONDON SE10 9NF.   Tel.081 858 4422 extn 6722

National Register of Archives
Quality House, Quality Court, Chancery Lane, LONDON WC2A 1HP.   Tel. 071 242 1198

Post Office Archives
Freeling House, Mount Pleasant District Office, LONDON EC1A 1BB.   Tel. 071 239 2570

Public Record Office
Chancery Lane, LONDON WC2A 1LR.   Tel. 081 876 3444

Public Record Office
Ruskin Avenue, Kew, RICHMOND, Surrey TW9 4DU. Tel. 081 876 3444

Rural History Centre
Institute of Agricultural History, University of Reading, PO Box 229, White Knights READING, Berks RG6 2AG. Tel 0734 318666

Society of Genealogists
14 Charterhouse Buildings, Goswell Road, London EC1M 7BA. Tel. 071 251 8799

South Wales Miners Library
University College of Swansea, Hendrefoilan House, Sketty, SWANSEA SA2 7NB. Tel. 0792 201231

Scotland

Business Archives Council of Scotland
Glasgow University Archives & Business Records Centre, 13,Thurso St, GLASGOW G11 6PE. Tel. 041 339 8855 extn 6494

Companies House (Scotland)
100-102, George St, EDINBURGH EH2 3DJ. Tel. 031 225 5774

Companies House (Glasgow Branch)
21, Bothwell St, GLASGOW G2 6NR. Tel. 041 248 3315

Glasgow University Archives and Business Records Centre
The University, GLASGOW G12 8QQ. Tel. 041 330 5516

National Register of Archives (Scotland)
Scottish Record Office, West Register House, Charlotte Square, EDINBURGH EH2 4DF.

Scottish Brewing Archive
Glasgow University Archives and Business Records Centre, The University, GLASGOW G12 8QQ. Tel. 041 330 5516

Scottish Industrial Heritage Society
Honorary Secretary, Eric T. Watt, 129, Fotheringay Rd, GLASGOW G41 4LG

The Centre for Business History in Scotland
Glasgow University, 4, University Gardens, GLASGOW G12 8QQ.
Tel. 041 339 8855 extn 4726

Northern Ireland

Public Record Office of Northern Ireland
66, Balmoral Avenue, BELFAST BT9 6NY.   Tel. 0232 661621/663286

Registry of Companies and Friendly Societies (N. Ireland)
IDB House, 64, Chichester St, BELFAST BT1 4JX.   Tel. 0232 234488

Ireland

Companies Registration Office
Dublin Castle, DUBLIN 2.   Tel. (01) 614222

Irish Manuscripts Commission
73, Merrion Square, DUBLIN 2.   Tel (01) 761610

National Archives of Ireland
Bishop St, DUBLIN 8, Eire.   Tel.0103 531 783711

Isle of Man

Companies & General Registry
Finch Rd, DOUGLAS, Isle of Man.   Tel. 0624 685233

7. Further Reading

General

Bibliography of British Business Histories
Francis Goodhall, Gower, 1987.

Business Archives as a Source for Family History
Mair Davies, Genealogists Magazine June 1964.

Business Documents, their Origins, Sources and Use to the Historian
John Armstrong & Stephanie Jones, Mansell, 1987.

Company Archives – A Survey of the Records of 1000 of the First Registered Companies in England & Wales
Gower, 1986.

Company Records as a Source for the Family Historian
C.T. & M.J. Watts, Genealogists Magazine , June 1983.

Debrett's Bibliography of Business History
Stephanie Zarach (Ed.), Macmillan, 1987.

Dictionary of Business Biography Vols 1-5
(Over 1000 biographies of British Business Leaders 1860 to 1980), Editor, David J. Jeremy, Butterworths, 1984.

Dictionary of Scottish Business Biography 1860-1960
Editors, Anthony Slaven and Sydney Checkland, Aberdeen University Press 1986, (Vol I) & 1990 (Vol II).

Directory of Corporate Archives , 3rd Edn
Lesley Richmond & Alison Turton, Business Archives Council, 1992.

Directory of British Associations & Associations in Ireland
Editors, G.P. & S.P.A. Henderson, CBD Research Ltd, Edn 11, 1992.

Guide to Tracing the History of a Business
John Orbell, Gower, 1987.

Londoner's Occupations: A Genealogical Guide
Stuart A. Raymond, Federation of Family History Societies, 1994.

Occupational Sources for Genealogists: A Bibliography of Printed Materials, Stuart Raymond, Federation of Family History Societies, 1992.

Registration of Companies & Businesses
Public Record Office Records Information Leaflet No. 54, June 1990.

The Early Scottish Limited Companies 1856-1895
P.L. Payne, Scottish Academic Press, 1980.

The Nature of Business Records – Record Aids No.4
Tony Cole, Business Archives Council.

The Uses of Business Archives – Record Aids No.2
John Orbell, Business Archives Council.

Specialist

Banking
A Guide to the Historical Records of British Banking
L.S.Pressnell & John Orbell, Gower, 1985.

Lloyd's Bank in the History of Banking
R.S. Sayers, Oxford University Press, 1957.

Bankrupts
Alphabetical List of All Bankrupts 1 Jan 1774-13 Jun 1786
J. Jarvis, London 1786.

Complete Register of all Bankrupts 1820-1843
George Elwick, Simpkin Marshall & Co., 1843.

Brewing
The Brewing Industry: A Guide to Historical Records
Lesley Richmond and Alison Turton, Manchester University Press, 1990.

The Brewing Industry in England 1700-1830
P. Mathias, Cambridge University Press, 1959.

Essex Brewers and the Malting and Hop Industries of the County
Ian P. Peaty, Brewery History Society, 1992.

Coventry
Register of Business Records of Coventry & related areas
Joan Lane, Lanchester Polytechnic, 1977

Directories
British Directories 1850 - 1950
Gareth Shaw & Allison Tipper, Leicester University Press, 1989.

Guide to the National & Provincial Directories of England & Wales, excluding London, published before 1856
Jane E. Norton, Royal Historical Society, 1950.

The London Directories 1677-1855
C.W.F. Goss, Denis Archer, London, 1932.

Inventions
New and Improved: Inventors and Inventions that have changed the modern world
R. Baker, HMSO 1976.

Insurance
The British Insurance Business, 1547 - 1970
H.A.L. Cockerell & Edwin Green, Hieneman Educational, 1976.

Iron & Steel
The British Iron & Steel Industry, 450 BC to AD 1775
H.R. Schubert, Routledge & Keegan Paul Ltd, 1957.

Latin America
Latin-American Business Archives in the U.K.
D.C.M. Platt, A. & C. Black 1965.

Newspapers
Local Newspapers 1750-1920 – in England, Wales, Channel Islands & Isle of Man
Jeremy Gibson, Federation of Family History Societies, 1991.

Railways
Was your Grandfather a Railwayman? – Directory of Railway Archive Sources for Family Historians
Tom Richards, Federation of Family History Societies, 1989.

Record Repositories
Family History Sources
Post Office Archives, 1987.

Guide to the Modern Records Centre
University of Warwick Library, 1986.

Handlist of Business Archives at the Guildhall Library
Joan Bullock-Anderson
Corporation of London, 1991.

Tracing your Ancestors in the PRO – Section 45, Business Records
Amanda Bevan & Andrea Duncan
HMSO, 1991.

Shipping & Shipbuilding
Shipping – a Survey of Historical Records
Peter Mathias & A.H.W. Pearsall
David & Charles, 1971..

The Shipbuilding Industry - A guide to historical records
Editor L.A. Richie
Manchester University Press, 1992.

Modern British Shipbuilding: a guide to historical records
L.A. Ritchie
National Maritime Museum 1980.

Textiles
Records of British Business & Industry, 1760 - 1914: Textiles & Leather
HMSO, 1990.

The Ulster Textile Industry: a catologue of business records in the Principal Registry of Northern Ireland (PRONI)
PRONI, 1978.

The West Riding Wool Textile Industry: a catologue of business records from the 16th to the 20th Century
1975.

Periodicals
Business Archives, Journal of the Business Archives Council.

Business History, published by Franks Cass .

Business History News, Newsletter of the Association of Business Historians..

Scottish Industrial History published by the Scottish Industrial Heritage Society.

Construction History, Journal of the Construction History Society.

Accounting Business & Financial History edited by John Richard Edwards of the Cardiff Business History Research Unit and published by Routledge, Cheriton House, Northway, ANDOVER, Hants SP10 5BE..

The Local Historian, Quarterly Journal of the British Association for Local History.

Index